Pretty Nostalgic

HOME

HAPPY DAYS FROM
VINTAGE WAYS

Pretty Nostalgic

HOME

NICOLE BURNETT & SARAH LEGG

PUBLISHED BY PRETTY NOSTALGIC LTD, WALES

A Pretty Nostalgic® publication
Copyright © Pretty Nostalgic® LTD 2012

Duke of Wellington Mews, Church Street,
Cowbridge, Vale of Glamorgan, South Wales, CF71 7BB

prettynostalgic.co.uk

First published in the UK 2012

Text copyright © Nicole Burnett and Sarah Legg 2012

Nicole Burnett and Sarah Legg have asserted their rights to be
identified as the authors of this work in accordance with the
copyright, designs and patents Act, 1988.

A catalogue record of this book is available from the British Library
and the National Library of Wales.

Vintage postcards and illustrations © Copyright Nicole Burnett 2012

ISBN 978-0-9571339-0-7

Printed in Wales by Stephens and George
Concept: Nicole Burnett and Sarah Legg
Text: Nicole Burnett
Styling: Nicole Burnett and Sarah Legg
Design: Daniel Lewis, Lagrafica
Editor: Joanna Keeling

LIST OF CONTENTS

Happy Day's

Vintage Home Store   Artisan Market

Traditional Tea Room   happydayshomestore.co.uk

10

Foreword

WELCOME TO OUR FIRST PRETTY NOSTALGIC PUBLICATION –
PRETTY NOSTALGIC HOME

We are Nicole Burnett and Sarah Legg. We work together as vintage dealers and, even though we have very different backgrounds (Nicole was a museum curator and Sarah has had many jobs including nursing and sales), we have both been living "pretty nostalgic" lives, in our own ways for many years. Since joining forces and opening our own vintage shop, Happy Days, we have become convinced that it is a successful, satisfying and sustainable way of living.

We both live happily in a semi-traditional way, taking the best from the past and combining it with the most worthy aspects of our modern world. We are not, by any means, perfect – we are learning all the time – but we do make an effort to focus on what is really important for our families, our homes and for ourselves and refuse to be dictated to by the modern world.

Vintage has become a popular decorating style in recent times, so much so that factories have started mass producing artificially-aged vintage home wares to meet the demand. But vintage is so much more than a style; it is a way of life. It honours the ways of past generations, cherishes the wisdom of times gone by and appreciates what really matters.

We hope that this book will inspire you to look at the way you view your home and how you live in it. We want you to be able to furnish your home with things you love and things that will last, to create a home that makes the best of what you have and brings out the best in you – a home unlike any other, of which you can be proud.

It won't cost the earth, or put you into debt. It will be a happy home, one in which you will feel comfortable and relaxed. A home that you will want to share, and in which you will create and preserve wonderful memories.

Wishing you a
very happy home

Nicole and Sarah.

MAY ALL HAPPINESS BE YOURS

This is my special place

" My corner of the living room in the 1930s semi I share with my husband Jason and sons Archie, 9 and Ollie, 6. No boys' toys are allowed into my corner.

"I keep my most recent book purchases on the shelves. When I have finished poring over them they move into my study, soon to be replaced by the many other books I avidly collect (it is an addiction).

"On the shelves, you'll also find many other special bits and pieces – a forever changing display of family photos and little treasures I have found. See the beautiful vintage children's shoes I bought from eBay.

"The wall is my personal gallery space, which includes a drawing by my husband and some beautiful Victorian prints (I am passionate about Victoriana).

"My leather armchair is the most comfortable in the world. I bought it from the owners of our previous house for £20. I have prettied it up by wrapping an old, but beautiful, floral linen curtain around the seat cushion (I can change it according to mood and season – or when the dog has spent too much time on it). On the chair is a lovely cushion, which Sarah made for me from old pieces of Welsh blanket, an embroidered cushion cover found in a charity shop, and a Welsh tapestry blanket that was given to my mother by her grandmother for her bottom drawer.

"The early 20th Century oak table with barley twist legs is really a cutlery box. The top lifts to reveal a handy compartment, within which I keep my laptop and any bits of technology that need to be kept out of the way, but within reach.

"The raspberry coloured rug with cream roses was a fantastic charity shop find, as it was mistaken for a throw and priced at just £4. And I love it"

Nicole

This book is not about decoration and interior styling. It is about how you can furnish and live in your home to make it the happiest it can be.

Happy days from vintage ways

Each chapter of this book is inspired by a proverb – words of wisdom that were founded on experience and handed down through the generations.

Even though we are familiar with some of these today, many have lost their potency and meaning. But as we become increasingly disillusioned with modern ways of living, then perhaps reminding ourselves of those old rules can help us to live happier and more fulfilling lives.

How often do we hear stories of how people in the past were poor but happy? Why is it then that we can feel so dissatisfied when we have so much?

Are we are in danger of living such complicated lives, so overloaded with possessions, that we have no time for the simple pleasures in life?

Some people create beautiful homes, in which not even they can feel comfortable – homes that have cost the earth in many ways, using up the planet's and their families' own resources without check, only to be just as dissatisfying and soulless at the end as they were at the start.

We live in a strange world; the more we have, the more we seem to want. We are willing to accept poor quality, expensive goods as quick fixes to fulfill our desires and not even mind when they don't last very long, as by then we have spotted something else we want to replace them with. We confuse our own desires and identify them to ourselves as real needs. Our focus is often on the silly and the superficial and many of us will look back on our money and consumer driven lives and wonder if it was really worth it.

But it doesn't have to be this way.

HAPPY DAYS BE THINE

HOME SWEET HOME

happy memories whenever you look at them.

Look at your home – do you love it?

Do you enjoy spending time alone in it?

Do you love sharing it with family and friends and, just as importantly, do they love sharing it with you?

If you had to stay housebound for a year in your home, how would you manage?

And would you continue to enjoy it?

* **Does it have all the fixtures and fittings a house requires?**
* **Does it function well?**
* **Is it filled with items you need, which function as well as they should?**
* **Does it give you pleasure, and fill you with pride?**
* **Is it full of beautiful things?**
* **Does it bring back memories?**
* **Does it identify you and mean something to you?**

If the answer to any of these is no, then why? It is your home nobody else's and everyone deserves a home they are happy with and can be happy in.

Being pretty nostalgic is about continuing a way of life founded long ago and following the principles and ethics of our ancestors, whilst still living in the modern world. It's about not allowing mass media, fat cat companies and advertising executives to tell us how we should live and how our homes should look.

We can go back to the good old days – we just need to focus on what was good about them!

Your home should give you a warm glow inside. Just the thought of it should invoke memories of loved ones and friends, good times, good food, comfort and security.

A home cannot be bought from a catalogue; it needs to evolve as a reflection of your achievements and triumphs. Your family's heirlooms, treasures made by your children, photographs of loved ones, the interesting items you have been given, found, bargained for or crafted yourself are a testament to you and those around you. They are talking points for your guests, potted histories of your life and triggers that allow you to play back

HOME MEANS YOU

I'm feeling fine and work-
ing hard.
But always have in view
The goal of getting home
again
For that means YOU.

HAPPY FACES. [*Drawn by ROBERT BARNES.*]

"Fair, happy faces, and a loyal wife: | One tune amid the treacherous chords of life,
Whose pulses never beat | Unchanging, true, and sweet."

People in the past would have found this particular maxim a lot easier to follow than we do today. They were taught to be grateful with their lot and that there was no point wasting effort on grand ideas, which could never be afforded or achieved. They believed that: "What cannot be cured must be endured," and just got on with their lives.

We are much more fortunate today. We are told that anything is possible but, as inspiring as this can be, it can also create an insatiable "I want" attitude to life.

Our over publicised and over stimulated media driven lives make it virtually impossible to ignore the wonderful possibilities out there for our homes. Everyone can see what you have or what you haven't got and we judge ourselves against some pretty impressive role models, seen on screen, in shops and books and magazines.

But we cannot possibly have it all, or even try to keep up to date with the latest trends and must-haves. Especially as things today go out of date almost as soon as they are made. It is a pointless pursuit, which will not lead to a happy home.

count your blessings

My Wish

May ne'er a day go by
Without a sunbeam in the sky;
And ne'er a day come to an end
That is not gladdened with a friend.

MANY HAPPY DAYS

Appreciate those around you
– family, friends and neighbours
– always make them welcome in your home and
gratefully accept offers of help.

If people didn't want to help they wouldn't offer.
Helping each other makes our relationships
stronger, as everyone needs to feel appreciated
and useful.

> "The charm of every house is to find the people in it self-contained, and taking their pleasure and comfort where they can, in the things that come to them, rather than in what they have had to seek painfully for"
>
> The House Beautiful, Clarence Cook, 1877

We would hate you to think we wanted to keep people down and stop them aspiring for better things, as we truly believe that anything is possible and that anything can be achieved. Today there are no restrictions to what people can and cannot have, but we want you to focus first on what you do have.

As, often, what we most crave is no better than what we have already.

This couple, setting up home during the Second World War, had little chance of getting everything they needed for their home, and no chance of getting all they wanted. But they would have appreciated the concept of counting your blessings. They would have been helped by their family and friends and they would have made the most of any resources they had.

During the Second World War, people had no choice but to make the most of what they had and what they could get hold of, and this led to an amazing spirit of invention and lateral thinking in homemaking.

> "Already homes show more originality, more individuality, than they did in pre-war days... no suites, no reproduction of model rooms in furnishing stores but an assembly of only essential articles of furniture, widely apart in their origins, yet combining harmoniously to produce an atmosphere of ease and home likeness"
>
> The ABC of Homemaking. Isabel Horner 1949.

Whether you live in the house of your dreams or the house of your nightmares, focusing on the positives will make it easier to live with the negatives.

Make the best of the house you live in, the size of the rooms, the fixtures and fittings and the furniture you have.

Don't let any wonderful feature go unnoticed.

Make an inventory of your worthwhile assets.

Compile a list of any quirky original features.

If you have a fireplace, then open it up and get it working.

Do you have an original wooden floor lying beneath an old carpet?

Are the largest and lightest rooms being used for the best purposes?

making the best of it

Helen resisted the temptation to replace her old bathroom suite. Instead she has accessorised it with old enamel items, making a quirky yet functional period bathroom.

A little thought has made the best of this awkward downstairs bathroom, saving the expense of an extension to the house.

Brett and Wayne have made the most of a sunny window overlooking their lovely garden by installing a window seat.

Jayne removed the wall separating the back room in her cottage by the sea, opening up the stairs and increasing the light and feeling of space.

Solid items such as this Victorian washstand are wonderful things. Although not required for their original purpose, they make beautiful pieces of furniture and can be used as sideboards and for storage in any room of the house.

Laura rescued this lovely aged wooden framed mirror from a family shed, just before it went into a skip.

Granny's best china often lived in a cupboard for all its life, only coming out for christenings and Christmas. Get these lovely old tea sets out. Display them and use them — there is nothing nicer than having tea from a proper cup and saucer.

If you are lucky enough to inherit a lovely old country piece such as this antique elm Windsor chair, give it pride of place as it is like inviting your ancestors who once sat in it into your home as guests.

I don't know when I shall be able to play at dolls again for all the things are put away in a box;

Except Jemima and the pestle – and-mortar, and they're in the bottom drawer with my Sunday frocks.

Many of us have relatives with old but sturdy pieces of family furniture hidden away. Chest of drawers such as this were often moved into the garage in the 1950s and 60s when they went out of fashion   time to rediscover them.

Taking stock

What furniture do you have? What can you acquire through family and friends? Do ask – many people will be delighted to find a worthy home for something they no longer need but don't want to throw away.

It is a real blessing to have solid and well-constructed furniture and, even if you don't like the way it looks now, its appearance can be changed for the better and it will remain useful almost indefinitely. Take a look at some of the furniture transformations in the next chapter...

Many of our customers at Happy Days, who admire and buy our vintage wares, later go on to explain how they have boxes of similar things in their shed, which belonged to their granny. They just don't appreciate what they have. If they sorted out granny's boxes, they would probably find all kinds of beautiful and reusable treasures, far nicer than anything they could buy – and they would all have a personal connection to their own past.

Life is like a blanket that's too short. Pull it up and your toes are cold, push it down and your shoulders shiver. Clever people learn to draw their knees up, snuggle up, and enjoy a comfortable night...

Count your blessings and make the most of what you have!

Waste Not
Want Not

An old biscuit tin acts as a sewing box, filled with bobbins, buttons and sewing bits, while pins are stored in a recycled tobacco tin. Buying a special button box would have been an alien concept to most housewives, who just expected to use what they had.

Vintage mending kits – Don't Despair Just Repair.

WASTE NOT WANT NOT

Don't buy something new unless you have to.

Recycle, reuse, repair, mend and make do!

Mending Day

HOW quickly children's clothes
   will rip and tear!
   Each time I put off mending till
      so late,
I re'lize that a family of eight
   Can give a loving mother lots
      of care.
If more get born I really do declare
I'll put 'em into bed and make
   'em wait.
My brother hopes to learn to
   operate,
   But there is not a child that I
      would spare.

HE'S borrowed three that he
   pertends are dead.
   But I won't even think of such
      thin'!
And yet at mending time I've
   often said
   I almost wished—though p'raps
      it is a sin—
That God has sent *some* paper
   dolls instead
Whose clothes are only painted
   on their skin.

   —Burges Johnson.

WANTED! PAPER METAL·BONES

It is impossible to go back to how things were in the past – we don't need to save for everything we buy and we don't have rationing or shortages. The flood gates have been opened and the exciting and easily accessible world of modern consumables has been exposed.

Shopping has become our national pastime, and spending money we don't always have on new things we don't really need has become a habit – and it's a habit that's hard to break.

Almost all households today can furnish their homes cheaply and quickly from the high street, and often without paying any money up-front.
We seem to be forever buying items for our homes and this is not just because of our craving for new things, but because we live in a society where it is cheaper to buy new items than it is to mend old ones. Many products, in fact, are designed not to last and to be unrepairable, even if the spare parts could be found.

These vintage tins and metal containers are just as useful today as when first made. Some were used as they were and some redecorated or the metal reused to make something else. Perhaps if our modern packaging were as substantial, we would be able to reuse it too, which is more sustainable than melting things down and recycling them into something new.

Decorated Tins

Fig. 298.

These vintage lovers are learning new skills at a Make-Do-and-Mend workshop at the Vintage Festival at Royal Festival Hall, July 2011.

Fig. 290.—Overmantel, with Pillars of Cotton-reels.

If you change the way you look at the things you own, and search out the real value of your old possessions, you will learn to appreciate qualities other than shiny newness.

By developing a waste not want not mentality, we can save money, help the environment and have uniquely different and praiseworthy homes.

Today, before you recycle, make sure you are not getting rid of anything you could use. These pieces of pretty card were cut from an old cake box and used to make gift tags (the ribbon came from the hanging loops sewn into the shoulders of new clothes). It is silly to put stuff in the recycling and then the next day spend good money on buying something someone else has taken seconds to make out of the same materials.

People in the past made all sorts of things out of rubbish. Bobbins were particularly useful – this large industrial bobbin was converted into a bobbin holder. With a bit of know-how you could even make a lovely shelf unit from old bobbins.

No packaging was thrown away even cotton flour bags were a valuable source of fabric. This one was used as stuffing in an old cushion. During the war, people used to make items from tea towels, children s clothes and curtains.

If you don't like a piece of furniture – you can change it.

Sarah bought this 1940s sofa on eBay and recovered it with her treasured collection of vintage fabric remnants.

This old wooden wardrobe was built to last and provides useful storage. Painting it white transforms it into a desirable bedroom piece.

This comfy old chair has been recovered in a hand knitted wool cover.

This tatty armchair has been given a new life by being reupholstered in vintage Welsh wool blankets, which are beautiful, hard-wearing and naturally fire-retardant.

This beautiful early 20th Century glazed front bookcase wouldn't be first choice for most modern homes. After painting and distressing it in a pale grey it has been given a new lease of life. The pale colour allows it to fit with most colour schemes.

This not so old, yellow pine cupboard has been transformed with a coat of paint, a bit of distressing and by replacing the centre panel with chicken wire.

Reuse something old rather than just taking the easy option and buying new.

If you are unhappy with anything in your home, or you need a particular item, you don't have to automatically buy new. Look at what you've got, forget what things are and think instead about what they could be.

Because we are so detached from the process of making things, the methods and materials of construction are being lost to us.

Media and advertising makes us think we have to buy everything purpose-made, when often we can make something new out of items we already have.

This lime green tea cosy was made from the neck of a polo neck jumper, which was bought at a scout jumble sale for 10p. The jumper was boil-washed to felt it and then both arms were turned into cute wine bottle covers and the body section was turned into a cushion cover.

Old stoneware jars make wonderful toilet brush holders. They are stable and can be sterilised with boiling water. A wooden bristle toilet brush also looks much nicer than a modern plastic one.

The unusual vase in Nicole's living room is actually a broken lamp base and the flowers sit in a cut-down plastic lemonade bottle inside.

This old cutlery table makes great storage for a laptop and adaptors.

These pretty china flowers were rescued from a broken ornament and placed in this little glass vase (this vase was given to Nicole by her great aunt, it was the first thing her aunt bought after starting her first job in 1928 at the age of 14).

Helen has stacked old fruit crates and wine boxes in her hall to store all the shoes, hats and gloves belonging to her four children.

This old suitcase has been turned into a coffee table by fitting a plank top. You could also fit casters to the bottom so it is easy to move around good for magazines or children's toys.

One option is to wrap your items in fabric. It's easier on smaller items such as chairs or lamps, but it's well worth it — the effect can be amazing.

Old suitcases look great stacked on top of a wardrobe and are the perfect storage for seasonal clothes.

Sam has used old wooden crates to make storage shelves in her office.

This unusual wooden window frame has been transformed by being re-glazed as a mirror.

The reason our ancestors cherished their patchwork quilts and looked after them with such care was not just because of their function and beauty. These works of art, handcrafted over many months, contained the keys to many wonderful memories. Pieces of childhood clothing, mother's best blouse, curtains from the bedroom or granny's apron – each patch represented a small piece of history. A quilt made from new fabric could never recreate this personal attachment.

"It comes then, to this. If we wish to prevent waste, we must take the first steps towards it in our homes, and make the most of the materials at our command."

Girls Own Cookery Book 1880 Phyllis Brown

"Never waste or throw away anything that can be turned to account."

Mrs Beeton's Book of Household Management 1864

You shouldn't need to buy expensive off-the-roll material - just have a look at all the many different types of material you have around you which could be reused:

A beautiful old patchwork bedspread – an evocative reminder of the waste not want not way of life and an archive of beautiful fabrics.

The blinds in Sam's conservatory are made from odd but coordinating fabric pieces.

Clare makes her living from making beautiful items from recycled Welsh blankets.

This quilt was made with love for Rhian Willment by Nanna Jean 20.09.01.

This lovely heirloom patchwork quilt, made by somebody's Nanna Jean, was given to a charity shop! Sarah snapped it up and it now sits on her son's bed.

A modern patchwork project has turned scraps into a sweet dog.

Don't buy new material for patch working – it defeats the point. These scraps were cut out of old clothes and curtain fabric found around the house.

Years ago, many items were delivered in sacks and these precious sources of material were kept to be reused. Sacks made up the foundation of rag rugs. Many older people remember winter evenings cutting up strips of dad's old trousers and poking them through a bit of sacking to make a new rug.

Don't buy expensive versions of things you throw away. If you save old rags, you will never have to buy a dishcloth, duster or floor cloth again.

Nicole is fascinated with old methods of mending. This forms a small part of her collection of broken items, which show the many lost arts of repair, such as the riveting of china.

This beautiful, hand painted antique plate hangs on Nicole's kitchen wall. It was broken over 100 years ago and riveted and is still going strong today.

"A mended plate lasts as long as a new one"

Older items were often made from quality materials, and constructed with more care than new mass-produced ones. With a little time and effort, they can be repaired or recycled and such personal achievements makes us love these items even more.

Every housewife would have once had a darning mushroom or egg in her sewing box and would have practiced the lost art of darning. There was no shame in using patched or darned items around the home, for it showed good domestic economy.

This collection of Carborundum products was used to keep tools sharp and in good working order. People in the past spent their time looking after and preserving their tools, rather than spending their weekends buying new ones.

Stick To It.

Copyright 1906 by M.T. Sheahan

GET A MOVE ON.

WHO NEVER TRIES CANNOT WIN THE PRIZE

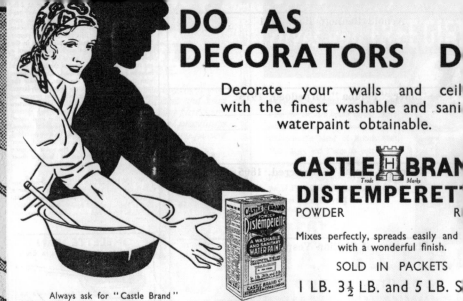

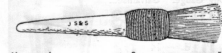

"If you have taste, perception, contrivance, and if you really enjoy having tasteful, pretty, beautiful things about you, you will somehow have them, but they will come out of yourself and will look like you and not like another."

The House Beautiful, Clarence Cook, 1877

You may not have heaps of sporting medals or trophies in your home, but each successful do-it-yourself project or handmade item you complete is your own personal triumph and a reward to be proud of.

With a little effort, your prize will be to have a house that is uniquely yours, which you can be justifiably proud of.

Making items for the home has almost become a middle class hobby rather than the necessary occupation it was years ago. It's often cheaper to buy new than to gather all the materials you need to make something – but are you getting what you pay for?

"proud homeowners have willingly recounted to me all that lay behind the contrivances, ingenuity, and planning, culminating in successful achievement, but what fun these home-makers have! Every item of furniture has its own history, and in it is invested with a value which cannot be assessed in terms of cash"

The ABC of Homemaking, Isabel Horner, 1949

If you ask your parents and grandparents about their first homes together, they will probably tell great stories of how they didn't have much to start with and made do with this and that and the wonderful ways they decorated their homes with the little they had. With no money to pay for labour, they would have done everything themselves or asked friends and family to help and when they think back, the pride and satisfaction of the things they made themselves would be hard to recreate today.

It is this personal investment that gives the most satisfaction and pride in a home.

WHO NEVER TRIES CANNOT WIN THE PRIZE

A handmade patchwork curtain helps stop draughts in this hallway.

1950s books and magazines provided lots of ideas for those homeowners willing to have a go at making things for themselves.

Man About the House

BY PETER HUNOT

HOME AND LEISURE

Home-Made GADGETS MAGAZINE

MONTHLY 1/-

THIS MONTH

MODEL AEROPLANE PILOT
RUSTY CAR-DOOR REPAIRS
A TROPICAL-TANK CLEANER
EASILY MADE KIDDIES' CAR
HOME-MADE AQUARIUM NET
NON-SLIP "HEX" SPANNERS
A USEFUL UNIVERSAL MOUNT
MOULD YOUR OWN ROCKERY
EASY-TO-MAKE ASHTRAYS
HOBBYISTS' HEXAGON WRENCHES
DEPENDABLE "FLAMMABILITY" TEST
AN ACCURATE CIRCLE-CUTTER
HOME-MADE PAPER PUNCH
A CAMERA-APERTURE GUIDE
and over FIFTY useful and novel
gadgets and devices for all purposes
10th Year of Publication

JAN. 1957
Vol. 10 No. 1

50 MONEY-SAVING DEVICES YOU CAN MAKE!

Have a go at painting – this amateur oil painting would grace any wall.

Beautiful needlework flowers on a vintage linen tablecloth

Close up of hand crochet daisy pattern on a homemade cot blanket.

A hand drawn cow on canvas by Sarah.

You could even paint your house!

Hours of work must have gone into this embroidered picture

42

You can easily change the look of a piece of furniture by replacing the handles and knobs. Nicole searches through a box of vintage china handles at the Salvo Fair to find the perfect one for this glazed bookcase.

Sarah makes teacup lamps from odd tea cups and saucers, drilled and threaded onto a standard lamp base.

Nicole made this sweet candle cup by melting down old candles.

Sarah made this pretty two-tiered cake stand from an odd tea plate and saucer — perfect for afternoon tea for one.

Linda went on an upholstery course so she could learn to reupholster her own furniture and this sofa is one of her amazing efforts.

A hand-embroidered cushion gets pride of place on the bed.

Jayne made this stair carpet by sewing a series of identical rugs together.

Anyone can hand sew simple decorations for the home, like this lavender heart.

44

Children should be encouraged to have a go too!

A simple peg angel, made from scraps.

This 1940s picture card game has been hand drawn onto old postcards and is stored in an old tobacco tin.

Children have incredible natural self-confidence and if they are encouraged to make things for themselves, from an early age, then they will grow up willing to have a go at anything.

This clever homemade strategy puzzle from the early 1900s has been carefully thought out and constructed.

This lovely 1930s chalk figure of a girl and her playful dog takes pride of place in Nicole's kitchen and is her constant reminder that "A Job Worth Doing is Worth Doing Well". It was to be the showpiece of her first ever shop display (a springtime theme of green and yellow vintage loveliness), but in her haste she carelessly threw the blanket that the figure was carefully wrapped in and knocked its head off. It has been restored, but still shows the damage as a reminder to Nicole that she needs to take more care and do a job properly from start to finish.

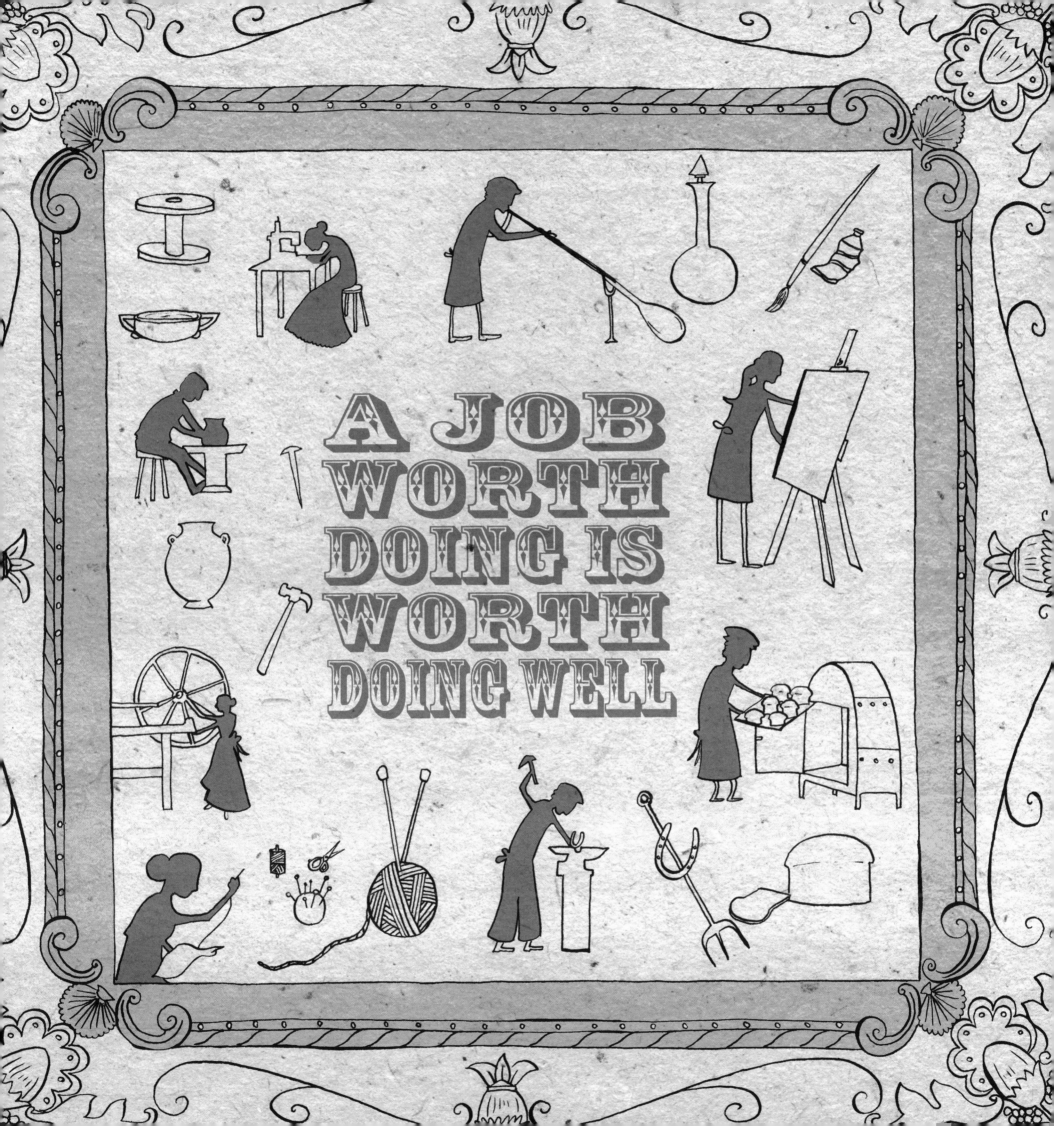

A JOB WORTH DOING IS WORTH DOING WELL

You don't have to buy cheap and nasty brass fittings from a DIY store. Seek out salvaged pieces, which were made to last (they don't even have to match). Or invest in a hand forged piece from an artisan maker.

This oak spoon holder was a wedding gift to Nicole and is now 15 years old. A craftsman made it using traditional methods and it is slowly darkening in colour as it ages. Unlike modern, mass-produced items, the older it gets the better it will look and the more valuable it will become.

Brett reused these old brass bath taps for his kitchen sink because they will continue to look this good forever. New taps just can't compete on looks, quality of materials or price.

If you need to buy a piece of furniture for storage – buy one that will last. This Victorian pine school cupboard was covered in layers of blue paint when bought, but worked out the same price as a similar MDF model. Once dipped and stripped, it looks better than new and its owners will never have to buy another one to replace it.

This period style light fitting was bought new from a small manufacturer. It is made from materials that will last and, although expensive compared to a plastic fitting, it adds the right finishing touch to a room.

A Job Worth Doing is Worth Doing Well

If this maxim were followed today, then most new homes and items of furniture would never be made. Our standards of craftsmanship and the quality of materials have undoubtedly faltered over the past few decades.

However, by choosing to recycle and reupholster old pieces of furniture, you can choose not to accept the many new, mass produced goods that flood our high streets.

Buy the best

"The rule that the best is the cheapest is the golden rule of furnishing. The chairs and tables are to be life-long friends, – the constant companions of the home-life- round which will cling the dearest associations, surely, then they should be honest and respectable chairs and tables, stay and stout-hearted, good types of their owners, like them ready to face the battle of life and do hard service therein"

Home Comfort, 1884

If you want to have quality items around you, then it is doubtful that you could afford to buy them all in one go.

Build up your collection slowly – keep an eye out for good items, buy them when you find them, negotiate reasonable prices and set them aside for later use.

Household linen used to be set aside and saved as part of a woman's trousseau or bottom drawer – most would remain a life long possession and then be passed down mother to daughter.

Artisan makers, restorers and crafters

There are still people out there who take real pride in their work and make and sell the best items they can – using quality materials and traditional methods and believing that if a job is worth doing it is worth doing well.

The Cooper:
A cooper making a barrel: a skilled craft, which takes many years to learn and produces beautiful items with years of use in them. They are costly compared with cheap imports, but if we don't invest in buying these handmade marvels, then they will stop being made.

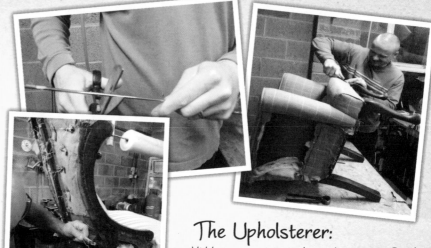

The Upholsterer:
Hidden away on an industrial estate in South Wales, Foy and Co employ a team of upholsterers with a detailed knowledge of their craft. A well-built antique sofa or chair was designed to be recoverable. For the same price as a cheap factory-built chair, you can buy a beautiful antique one and have it reupholstered and, chances are, the your recycled chair will far outlast a modern one. This upholsterer uses the best tools he can afford and looks after them by sharpening them by hand so they always give the best performance.

The Restorer:
Adam Jones is a furniture restorer, working in Cowbridge in South Wales. He can bring any well- built piece of furniture back from the brink and make it as good as new. Many of the pieces he works on are hundreds of years old but, with a bit of attention every half a century or so, they continue to provide good service over the generations. Antique furniture is real value for money, but we also have to invest in the people who can repair and look after them too. Adam can restore, repair or even replace bits of old furniture, like this drawer he has made to fit in this lovely little chest, making it useful once again.

The Furniture Maker:
Catherine Evans is part of a new generation of artisan furniture makers. She uses sustainable, native woods and crafts everything from little stools to entire kitchens. Most of her pieces are bespoke but amazingly cost no more than a quality factory piece from a high street store.

If you are no good with a sewing machine yourself – then find an independent soft furnishing maker. They will make curtains, cushions or anything else you want for your home, made to measure. They can even, if you wish, recycle and reuse material you already have – making it much cheaper than buying off-the-peg designer curtains.

The Basket Weaver:

Basket weavers make tactile items from locally sourced willow. They are sustainable and functional, but take time to make so the labour costs need to be covered in their retail price. However, once bought and if looked after, they will last for a long time and can be repaired if broken.

If you don't have the skill or confidence to tackle a job yourself and to do it well, then invest in someone who can. There are plenty of talented individuals who have dedicated to making hand crafted items and producing works of such a high standard, they could never be achieved by machines or in a foreign sweatshop.

Seek these people out – ask for recommendations from friends and family – because if they can't make a decent living doing what they excel at, then we are in danger of losing them.

Armorel Hamilton trained as an illustrator and now makes these amazing little creatures called Faybles™. You can commission her to make one to live in and protect your own home or as a special friend for a loved one. Every creature has a unique character and Armorel spends days channelling her energies into each one as she brings them to life. You won't find anything quite like this on the high street and special items like these are worth investing in for your home. They will be the things your children will remember and your future family heirlooms. They can seem expensive, but wouldn't you prefer to look at one of these than yet another electric gadget?

Helen's tiny garden is made more vibrant with the back of the house painted a dark raspberry pink.

Fortune Favours the Bold

A bowler hat light shade, made by Sophie Creed for her vintage clothing Boutique Ears and Whiskers.

You can be bold with everything in your house – even light fittings.

Important – make sure all electric fixtures and fittings are checked and installed by a qualified electrician.

Vintage aluminium jelly moulds make unusual light shades for a kitchen.

This French chandelier sits over a simple oak table in a rustic kitchen so really gets noticed.

Sarah made this teacup lamp, using a standard table lamp fitting, threaded with drilled cups and saucers.

Another of Sarah's lamp creations, this one made from a vintage soda syphon.

It's your house – go wild!

"The mind which blindly accepts fashions simply because they are fashionable, without trying to discriminate in what, the new is better than the old, may be said to resemble those caged reptilian jaws, champing without discretion flesh, feathers and blanket at once!"
The Art of Decoration, Mrs Hawes 1881.

Why are we forever spending vast sums of money so that our homes can look just like everyone else's? We seem to have lost the spirit of individualism and are afraid to be unique. It's your home – you must decorate it to suite your tastes and needs and also those who share it with you. So many homes today are unspectacular, with no real distinguishing features to tell them apart from the house next door.

Have the confidence to be bold and try something new. Flamboyance has little to do with money – it's all about experimenting, following your dreams and passions.

In recent years, we have seen many home fashions – from minimalism to modern retro and shabby chic – than any other era. You may love one, all or none of these fads but whatever your tastes, you don't have to follow fashions.

"Avoid the fatal sheep-walk which the timid and ignorant so soon beat out, the stereotyped house... to give our individual stamp to our own property in the common heritage of the beautiful"
The Art of Decoration, Mrs Hawes 1881

"If we ask where the old-time people found their models, we certainly do not get for an answer, that they sought the advice of this or that architect. Whatever they did, were it good or bad, came out of their own minds, and was suggested by their own wants, and represented their own taste and sense of fitness"
The House Beautiful, Clarence Cook 1877

"We ought to seek the individual expression of ourselves, of our own family life, our own ways of living, thinking, acting, more than doing as other people are doing, more than the having of what other people are having"
The House Beautiful, Clarence Cook, 1877

"Dare to be original and to express yourself, at all costs avoid being a mere copyist"
The ABC of Homemaking, Isobel Horner, 1949

Armorel Hamilton's magical stag on her living room wall.

Helen made a collage of old maps to cover her bathroom wall. After a coat of varnish, they become resistant to water – as well as being educational whilst having a long soak.

Maggie uses an old washing dolly as a quirky loo roll holder.

Brett and Wayne fitted a huge salvaged Victorian glass window to one wall to let in lots of light.

Customise your cupboards

Laura uses an old string shopping bag to hold toilet rolls on the back of her cloakroom door.

Helen also uses an old washing implement, a copper posser, to hold her loo rolls.

A decorative carved wardrobe makes a striking addition to Leanne's modern kitchen.

Sam's collection of Victorian tiles has been used to wonderful decorative effect on her stairs.

Sarah painted this retro kitchen cabinet with the union jack to celebrate the wedding of Prince William and Kate Middleton. She kept it the following year to mark the Queen's Diamond Jubilee, however, it's easy to paint over again when a change is needed.

This Edwardian gentleman's armchair has been recovered in a random and contrasting collection of vintage Welsh blankets, but the boldness of the designs do work together.

The owners of this house were bold enough to chop down the legs of this old farmhouse kitchen table in order to make their coffee table.

Kept by the power of God.

Helen's stuffed wild boar is almost treated as one of the family.

For the People
IN POWDER
HUDSON'S
SOAP
¼ lb. PACKETS

HUDSON'S
No 1 2
Extract Soap

Old cane shop mannequins are beautifully formed and very decorative. In this sunny hall they cast elaborate shadows on the walls.

It's all in the display: have the confidence to show off your bits and pieces to their best advantage.

This carved, lime washed mirror looks great nonchalantly leaning against the wall, instead of being carefully hung on it.

Two lovely collections of incredibly different vintage finds, but they work together in a decorating scheme. Be brave and follow your instincts.

A
Thing of
Beauty is
a Joy
Forever

Pretty yet practical

You can choose functional items, which are beautiful to look at too.

A Thing of Beauty is a Joy Forever

This old saying, originally by John Keats, is probably one of the most important ideals to follow when turning a house into a home. You will get pleasure from looking at and using items you love, have a sentimental attachment to or you think to be beautiful, whether a pretty old jug or a portrait painted by one of your children. Don't hide away items that mean something to you - cherish and display them and they'll remind you of people and things which are important to you.

Nicole's favourite picture — an antique hand tinted engraving of a Victorian lady with a bowl of broth.

You should get pleasure even from looking at something as mundane as a light shade.

> In these days when economy in money, labour, and space is imperative, utility may have to be the first consideration, but it should not be the only one, for the soul needs beauty for its food
>
> The ABC of Homemaking, Isobel Horner, 1949

A beautiful home isn't necessarily a happy one - but there is no reason why a happy home can't be beautiful.

> The home should delight the eye as well as the heart. That light, colour and form have a direct influence on the mind and temper refining and brighten them
>
> The Art of Housekeeping, Mrs Hawes, 1889.

Vintage glass comes in lots of lovely colours, shapes and styles and is cheap to buy.

Look around your home - do the objects you live with have real beauty? Do they make you happy?

We should get real pleasure from the items we choose to have in our homes.

Don't buy a picture just to match your new curtains but buy one that lifts your spirits.

Items only have to be beautiful to you and those who live in your home. Beauty is very much in the eye of the beholder and we all have different tastes.

A beautiful jug decorated with pink roses — this might not be quite your cup of tea, but you are sure to find a jug that will please you to look at and use.

Surround yourself with beautiful things.

Beauty for Beauty's Sake

Why have things in your home that you do not like, make you sad or are ugly? If you don't like them — change them, swap them, update them or find them a new home.

A collection of beautiful treasures fill all the shelves in Helen's house.

A 1930s chalk figure of a little girl with an umbrella — a little faded and chipped but very endearing and loved by its owner.

A fairy called Snow-flake and a Fayble called Swamp Troll, both by Armorel Hamilton, sit on a frame made from old grape vines in Nicole's living room. "I absolutely adore these little creatures and appreciate them every day and will treasure them forever."

This sweet little bird ornament was bought at a boot sale for 50p.

Helen's collection
of vintage ebony
hand mirrors
sit on the
mantelpiece in
her bedroom.

Pieces of real china make afternoon tea in the garden extra special. The
teapot and milk jug are 1930s Melba Ware and the teacups are hand
painted with Fuchsia flowers and date to around 1820. Use and appreciate
lovely tea sets, they are beautiful to use and to look at.

**Maggie's collection of honey pots,
added to over the over the years,
makes a nice display on her dresser
and she takes it in turn to use them
at breakfast.**

Nicole's children
collect semi-
precious stones
and this printer's
tray is the perfect
place to display
them and other
bits they dig up
at the beach or in
the garden. They
also buy a different
gemstone from
their tooth fairy
money as little
souvenirs of their
childhood.

A.mEThuc.t

Learn patience...

...collecting items bit by bit is far more satisfying than buying
a whole collection in one go.

"Too much of a good thing is good for nothing."

Nicole collects vintage postcards, and many of them appear
in this book. "The excitement of discovering previously unseen
images with lovely photos, illustrations and colours gives me
lots of enjoyment and then I get to look at them forever."

Another of Nicole's collections
Victorian tiles dotted around the house.

This poor one-eyed push along dog is still a best friend to his owner.

It is worth buying your own children a beautiful pair of shoes like these antique examples, just to sit on a shelf and remind you just how tiny they once were as they grow too fast.

STEFAN

Amelia has just as much fun playing dollies with this vintage cot as the original owner did and it is much nicer to look at than a modern plastic one.

There is real beauty in a well-made toy, which had been looked after and yet well played with.

Amelia has inherited her mum's special childhood toys and mixes them with her own.

This colourful, hand knitted child s dress from the 1940s has become a family heirloom.

Encourage children to see the beauty in objects and give them things they will want to cherish for the rest of their lives.

This special childhood friend has been retired to a shelf, but she is no less loved.

This wooden doll has been named Evangeline by her latest owner and has been dressed in scraps of vintage linen and hand crochet lace with the original draper's tag still on.

INKDEATH

A childhood rocking horse, still has pride of place even in a grown-up's bedroom.

Vintage children's books, like this set of Enid Blyton books make a lovely display.

Some things are just too beautiful to use. Nicole bought this unused eiderdown cover at a boot sale for £2 to use in a craft project, but has decided she just can't cut it up and is happy to keep it as just a lovely piece of material. It has been used on the cover of this book.

Antique jugs have a special decorative quality and deserve to be appreciated and admired. They also make useful vases.

Always on display and used for special occasions, this pretty plate is more than just functional.

If you need a doorstop why not choose a cute little vintage kitten like this.

This plate displayed on the wall of Nicole's kitchen is as pretty as any picture.

Maggie bought this vintage pale pink enamel teapot decorated by a yellow rose as a present for a friend, but in the end she couldn't part with it.

The
Kitchen
is the
Heart
of the
Home

Helen's kitchen in her small railway workers' terrace has remained almost unchanged since it was built

The kitchen is the heart of the home

For the more well off families of the past, with a separate room for the kitchen, it could be a dull and lonely place of drudgery, especially when servants got better work offers and women were forced to work alone, away from the rest of the family. Although, it could be said, that some people today might appreciate the quiet solitude of those kitchens, as modern all-inclusive family kitchens don't offer any chance of escape and mean that all our kitchen activities are on constant public show.

What happens in the kitchen today is no longer the sole concern of the homemaker. The ins and outs of its running are often shared by everyone and the kitchen is not only for domestic duties, but it is a place to eat and a place to meet and even entertain — somewhere to do homework, get the sewing machine out or enjoy a jigsaw puzzle. It is, in many houses, the centre of the home and the place where we spend most of our time.

Nowadays the kitchen often has more money spent on it than any other room in the house. However, even with these wonderful new materials and appliances, we seem to be replicating the working class kitchens of the past. The back room, kitchen-cum-living room, where life centered round a glowing iron range, reflects the homely atmosphere of the kitchen as heart of the home, which we strive for today.

Leanne's modern family kitchen

Helen's kitchen is warmed on cold days by Rita, her trusty antique burner.

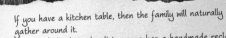
If you have a kitchen table, then the family will naturally gather around it.
In Jayne's kitchen, the dining area has a handmade reclaimed table and plenty of seating for family and friends on two old church pews.

SITTING AT THE TABLE

Many of us are guilty of letting our children eat dinner in front of the TV, but this should be the exception rather than the rule.

Family mealtimes were strictly adhered to in the past and they are still a priority in many countries of the world. In Britain, however, we have allowed these few fixed points in a family's busy schedule to be eroded. It's not uncommon for individual family members to pass like ships in the night with little idea what the others are up to or how they are feeling.

Try to eat a few family meals together in the week and enjoy the chance to catch up and share your lives with each other.

Helen and her family eat around an oak table in the back room next to the kitchen.

Children love homemade apple crumble — and as anyone with an apple tree will know, you get 10 in a row and then have to wait until the same time next year for more.

You can make yummy dishes quickly from the remains of the previous night's dinner — here are Laura's home made fish cakes made from left over cheesy mash, cooked salmon and a few herbs and breadcrumbs.

Bread and butter pudding — made from stale bread and fruit loaf, some home made jam, apples from the garden, a goose egg and some milk, butter and sugar. I didn't use a fixed recipe, just used what was at hand, and it was delicious! Don't be scared to experiment — you cannot go wrong with this sort of pudding.

Folks Must Be Fed

This little Queen of Hearts would have helped in making tarts from a young age, watching mother and then having a go herself. Who needs playdough?

THE IMPORTANCE OF COOKING

In the past, a mother's responsibility was to feed her family well. And for many housewives it became almost a full-time occupation, involving shopping for fresh produce every day and preparing a wholesome meal from scratch. It was hard work, but there were rewards – a table full of licked clean plates, delighted faces asking for seconds, to see your children growing up big and strong and a contented husband who invited work colleagues to dinner to show off his wife's cooking skills.

Few families would expect this sort of service today and few women would offer it. It is more common for everyone to take an active role in the running of the home, but perhaps a bit too many of the cooking duties have been delegated to the convenience food aisle of the local supermarket. Can we achieve the same levels of satisfaction from heating up a ready-made dinner?

It is healthier, cheaper and more satisfying to cook for your family and friends. You will have more control over what your children eat and can make sure they are getting a balanced diet. After all, cooking is what the kitchen is designed for.

Helen uses old shop weighing scales in her kitchen.

Nicole uses these Victorian scales for all her home weighing — they are perfectly accurate and a useful design.

A late Victorian Universal Food Chopper, designed to be screw fastened onto a pine kitchen table. This was mostly used to mince up left over cooked meat, which would be used in cottage pie or perhaps rissoles.

A 1950s Spong mincer in a lovely green. It has a suction base that allows it to grip to a Formica table, which was the wonder material of the 1950s — the easy to wipe surface was far easier to maintain than a pine table top.

Vintage Tala pastry cutters — practical, long lasting and the tin looks lovely on a shelf.

PASTRY CUTTERS

Old kitchen utensils often work better than new ones — they were built to last, and will perform for as long as you need them to. When you have finished with them, you can often sell them on for more than you paid for them in the first place.

Nicole's stoneware bread pan stores all her bread and rolls on the kitchen worktop. It was bought at a car boot sale for £25 but is worth much more.

A vintage aluminium colander will last forever.

A classic design – this vintage glass lemon squeezer will last for years and will happily go in the dishwasher too.

An ingenious 1950s pickle fork.

Old wooden chopping boards age gracefully over time and will last a long time as long as you don't put them in the dishwasher.

A sturdy Victorian potato ricer will get all the lumps out of your mashed potatoes.

This aluminium flour dredger, though at least 60 years old, looks as good as new and will provide endless years of service.

JAMS & JELLIES

HAVE A GO AT PRESERVING

Making jams, jellies and chutneys was an important kitchen job in the past. Gluts of seasonal fruit were preserved, so they could be used and enjoyed throughout the year and especially during the winter. Homemakers would feel an immense sense of pride looking in their larder at the rows of preserves and bottled fruit lined up, knowing that their family would have a good and varied diet all year round.

We can go to the supermarket and buy whatever we want whenever we want, but why not have a go at making your own preserves? It is not as hard as you think and they make great presents.

These damsons from the garden are being kept to be preserved, not as jam but Damson Gin a delicious way of using up a glut of fruit and a much appreciated gift.

Keep your eyes out for a good blackberry patch. These free fruits make lovely jams, jellies, puddings and cordials.

A cute pair of vintage preserve pots

A store of homemade jams and pickles

RECIPE
Blackberry and Brandy Christmas Cordial

Fill a large heavy bottomed saucepan with your blackberries.

For every 2lb of blackberries, add 1lb of sugar, the juice and grated rind of an orange, 1/2 a nutmeg grated. 1 oz of cloves, and a cinnamon stick. Simmer for 30 minutes and at the same time mash the berries to release the juice. Let the juice cool before adding the brandy to taste (around 1/2 pint)

Bottle and keep until Christmas, then strain before drinking, or use as it is on top of ice cream.

CREATE A FUNCTIONAL KITCHEN WITH CHARACTER

Make Meals Special

Put the ceremony back into mealtimes
Decorate the table and make it look attractive
Use the best china and crockery and enjoy it

Vintage plates are glazed with lead, so if they are crackled or crazed like this one then don t use them to serve food as the lead can leach out.

Hanging utensils keeps them within easy reach of the cook

Proper linen cloths are hard wearing.

Nicole keeps dishwasher cleaning tablets in her china duck pot.

A kitchen tea, using the blue and white china stored on the kitchen shelves.

Nicole's kitchen shelves with her collection of blue and white china, picked up in boot sales and charity shops.

Old glass jars are reused to store ingredients.

A 1950s kitchen cabinet is still useful in a modern kitchen and looks much nicer than a fitted kitchen unit.

Helen keeps her herbs and spices on vintage painted shelves over the cooker.

Jayne has very little worktop space or preparation area, but she combines storage with display, so that it looks more than just functional.

A traditional dresser provides plenty of easy to reach storage space. This family reuses old vintage tins and earthenware jars to store their modern ingredients.

A folding pine, wall-mounted rack stores a lot of plates in a small space. Don't worry about having matching sets of crockery — this kitchen just follows a mismatched blue and white theme.

This 1950s English Rose kitchen has been professionally restored and was being sold at the Salvo Fair. It has real character and looks so much nicer than an off the peg kitchen.

Wooden clothes driers can work well as hanging storage for pots and pans.

A painted reclaimed pine settle — the lift up seat is great for storage in a kitchen.

Make Time for Tea

Vintage French enamel coffee and sugar jars – a little bit bashed, but they still look great.

1950s midwinter tea strainer set – perfect for herbal teas.

1950s crinoline lady teapot

A plain and simple vintage teapot.

A vibrant green vintage teapot.

Unusual pink 1930s teapot

Having a drink of tea should be much more than just liquid refreshment. In the past, taking tea was an important ritual where family and friends took time out of their days to share in this once expensive commodity. Tea drinking was sociable and the tea itself was savoured, appreciated and much invested in.

Tea is not as costly as it once was and many of us now prefer coffee or other drinks instead, but we should still take time out in the day to enjoy a drink with someone.

So make time, stop what you are doing, boil the kettle, and get the teapot or coffee pot out. Leave the instant stuff in the cupboard and use the real thing instead – it will take a bit longer, but it will be worth it and, while you wait, you can chat or reflect on your day. Use nice china rather than any old mug and take a break instead of just sipping while you work.

Teatime (no matter what you choose to drink) should be a marker in your day, a rest point, a time to recharge yourself and a reward for your hard work.

Lovely jade green vintage butter knives they really do spread butter better than dinner knives try them.

It's a pleasure to choose a biscuit from this lovely sunny 1930s china biscuit barrel.

How can you not enjoy a cuppa from this?

Perfect for tea and biscuits in the garden or in front of the TV — a pretty vintage teacup with combined saucer and tea plate.

Pretty pink cherry blossom teapot

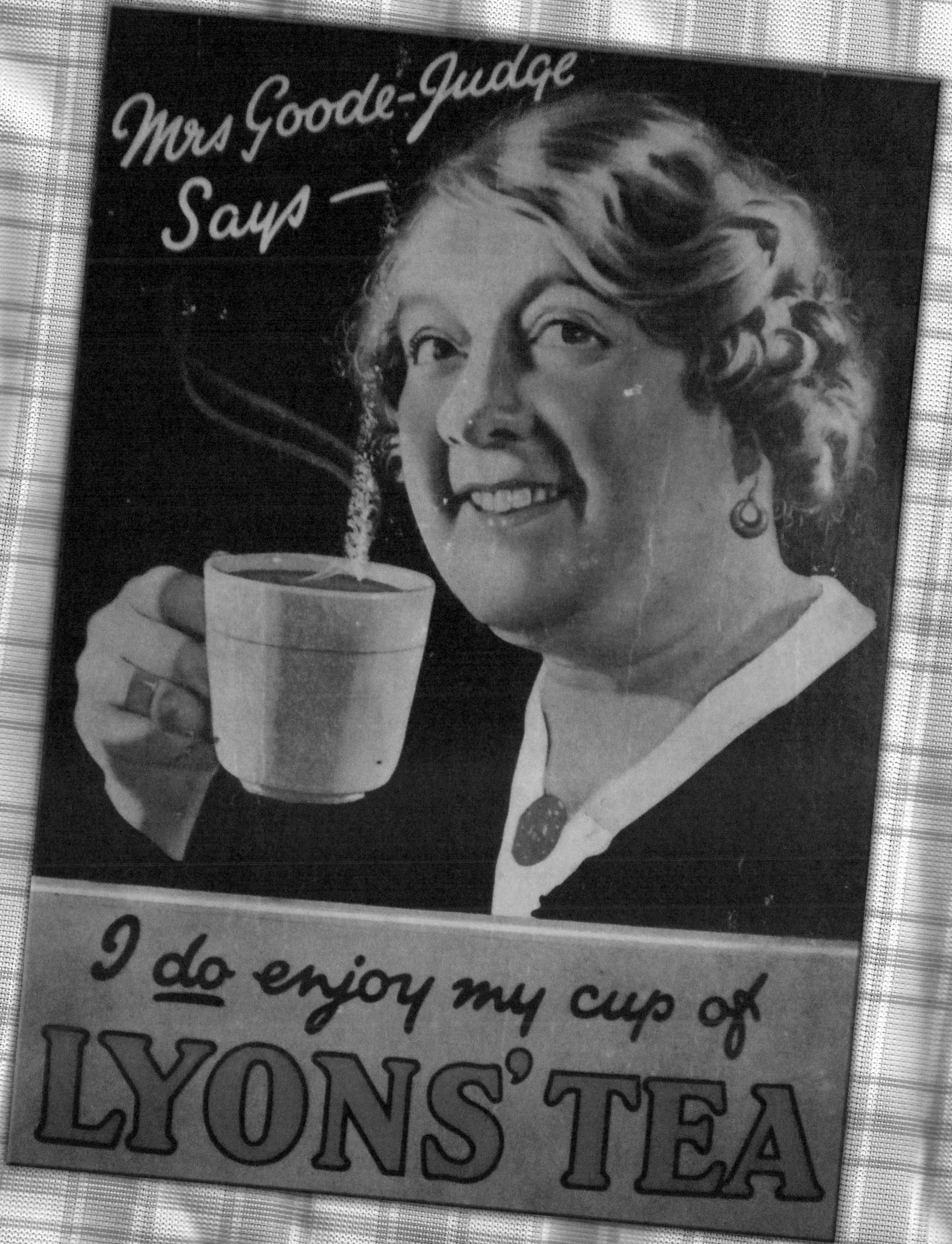
Mrs Goode-Judge
Says—
I do enjoy my cup of
LYONS' TEA

As we no longer work to the tune of the changing seasons, we are forgetting them. The only seasonal activities remembered by children nowadays are Christmas, Easter and Halloween and that's mostly due to the presents they receive.

We need to remember that — everything is good in its season.

If we mark each season as it changes, and live within its means, we will become more in tune with the world around us and time will pass in distinct stages rather than in one big unrecognisable rush.

People of the past didn't have the same minutiae concept of time. Instead of glancing at their clocks and watches every five minutes, they kept one eye on the sky and took notice of the changing seasons.

They lived by the phases of the moon, noting how it waxed and waned. From one new moon to the next, it is 29 and a bit days, roughly 4 weeks of 7 days. We still use the term fortnight, meaning 14 nights not days.

Each lunar period was associated with different agricultural activities, whether sowing seeds, haymaking, weeding, cutting corn or gathering fruit.

Our ancestors saw the year as an ever-turning wheel of changing seasons, where the sun grew strong and then became weaker, days lengthened and then shortened over and over again in a never-ending cycle.

Now we live indoors, in heated houses with artificial lighting, strictly observing timetables that we have created ourselves but that also stress us out. We are well aware that time flies, but often can't remember what we have done with it!

We are no longer reliant on growing our own food, but remembering and embracing the seasonal cycles of the earth within our homes can help us feel more grounded in our lives. It will help us to mark the passing of time whilst appreciating the wonders of Mother Nature and the fact that no matter how long the winter, spring is sure to follow.

AUTUMN

Picking the last of the year's harvest

Bulbs planted indoors in autumn will provide a lovely spring show.

AUTUMN.

A pot of damson butter given by a friend is a thoughtful gift

Damson butter

Autumn was marked as the New Year for our ancient pre-Christian ancestors.

Seen as the end of the light half of the year and the beginning of the dark half, autumn was also start of the resting period for the land and all creatures of the earth.

The last of the harvest was brought in and celebrated and produce was preserved and stored for use through the long, cold winter.

Our modern day Halloween originates from the pagan festival of Samhain, which has been celebrated for thousands of years. At this time, the veil between the living and the dead was said to be at its thinnest and people remembered lost loved ones by keeping a place for them at the table.

This was also the time of year when families made the tough decision as to which of their animals they could keep through the winter to breed from next year. For those who lived closely with their animals, it was like slaughtering faithful friends and so as a mark of respect to them and to thank the gods and bless the year to come there was a feast. A great fire was lit and the bones of the animals they had killed were tossed onto this bone-fire (later to become a bonfire). After the feast, the ashes from this bone-fire were scattered on the fields to bring luck to next year's crops.

Have a bonfire, no matter how small. Wrap up warm, bake some potatoes, toast marshmallows and drink mulled cider. You could even toss your leftover bones on the fire and use the ashes to fertilise your vegetable patch.

How to Celebrate Autumn...

Hold your own harvest festival
Feast on your own (or locally-bought) seasonal produce, make a bread plait or harvest loaf.

Carve a pumpkin or Jack'o Lantern
Once lit, it will keep unfriendly spirits from your door – or, rather, let every child in your neighbourhood know that your home welcomes trick-or-treaters.
Don't waste the inside of your pumpkins. Make pumpkin soup or pumpkin pie then toast the pumpkin seeds, which when sprinkled with salt and chilli flakes, make for tasty nibbles.

Take advantage of a glut of apples and do a bit of apple bobbing
Either float apples in a bowl of water, or tie them to string and dangle them from the door frame then, with hands behind your back, try to take a bite.

Tell a ghost story by candle light
Children and adults alike love to feel spooked by a good ghost story. Create the right atmosphere and it will be an event long-remembered by your audience.

Create something tasty that lasts through the winter
Make some blackberry jam, rosehip syrup, sloe gin or damson wine. Whatever autumn produce you can get hold of, find a way of preserving it so you can use it later in the year – or give it away as a present.

Play Conkers
Collect conkers and teach a child how to play. Many schools now don't allow conker fights so the championships of the past are purely adult affairs. Carefully make a hole through the conker with a screwdriver, thread through an old shoe lace or length of string, secure with a knot and you are ready for battle.

Find a sweet chestnut tree
British woodlands have many fine sweet chestnut trees with their lovely fruits there for the picking. Most of shop-bought chestnuts are imported and, although larger than our native chestnuts, they are no more tasty. You can roast them on a toasting fork in front of the fire, boil them or carefully microwave them after pricking them.

Bring an Autumn display into your home
A nature table with lovely red and gold leaves or a vase of bright berried branches will remind you every day what time of year it is.

Seek out seasonal touches to use in the home
An autumnal cushion cover, or tea cup. Find orange, gold, red and brown accessories and candles.

Prepare for winter – change the curtains
Now that the nights are drawing in and getting colder, change your curtains to cosier, dark-coloured, lined curtains to keep the draughts out and the heat in. Also, think about hanging door curtains or portieres on the main doors of the house – they look lovely and keep the house snug too.

Make your log pile
If you have a real fire or log burner, create space in your home to store your logs and coal. Logs can make a lovely display and it is great to know you are ready for all the wind, rain and snow by having enough logs stored inside.

Plant bulbs
If you plant spring bulbs indoors in autumn, you will have a wonderful display of perfumed spring flowers well before the garden and there is nothing like it to raise the spirits and show that winter is almost over.

Cooking over a bonfire

A lovely autumnal handmade crochet cushion

Helen clears a shelf in her dining room to store logs when the weather gets cold.

A harvest loaf, made in early autumn to celebrate the bringing in of the grain harvest.

Autumnal colours on a vintage cup and saucer.

Children's Halloween party

WINTER

Winters in the past could be harsh and a family's survival depended on the quality of the preparations they had made. Severe winters meant loss of animals and family members from sickness and hunger.

Winter can still be problematic for us today and because we do not lay down the kind of stores of supplies like people long ago, we are often caught short when the weather does turn on us. We are not self sufficient and if the lorries can't deliver goods to the shops, then we don't have anything to buy and our cupboards will quickly become bare.

We need to respect the seasons and the powers they have over us. If we prepare for the worst winter we can imagine and make our homes ready for the challenge of cold winds and freezing snow, then we can relax and be content and warm inside with all that we need to hand to ride the poor weather out.

WAITING FOR THE CRUMBS.

A Merry CHRISTMAS

With kindest Greetings for Christmas And all Good Wishes for your Happiness in the Coming Year.

A vast display of vintage Welsh blankets. So many colours and patterns were made that you are bound to find one to fit perfectly in your home.

Greetings and all Good Wishes

A cosy corner with a roaring fire, perfect for curling up to read on a chilly winter evening.

Enjoy the snow! Make a snowman, have a snowball fight, but don't forget to check on those less fortunate than you.

At Yule or the Winter Solstice, usually celebrated on December 21st, our ancestors celebrated the rebirth of the sun knowing that from then on the days would become lighter and the nights shorter. They could see the light at the end of the tunnel, so to speak, and so felt confident to use some carefully-kept supplies on a great feast.

This Yule feast later coincided with the Christian Church's celebration of Christmas but many seasonal pagan activities and traditions have been preserved and revived.

The Yule Log

The ceremony of dragging home the Yule Log was still practiced during Victorian times, especially in rural areas. Once placed in the fireplace, the log (traditionally oak, ash or pine) was lit from a burning piece of last year's log, which had been saved especially and was said to protect the house from fire.

In early Pagan times, the log had to burn for the whole of Yule and it would be decorated. Whilst it burnt, people would visualise the rebirth of the sun that shone amongst its flames and imagine the coming warmth of spring.

Festive Decorations for Winter

Vintage glass baubles have a subtle shine to them. Here, they add festive cheer to an antique brass plant holder, which hangs in a window.

Christmas trees lit with real candles look magical and were truly exciting for children of the past. Often the tree wasn't put up until Christmas Eve and so there was no chance of getting bored of the decorations before the great day.

Nicole prefers her living Christmas tree to sit on a table rather than on the floor. The table is laid with her treasured Victorian chenille cloth and the potted living tree, which is hung with a mixture of new, old, vintage and handmade ornaments, is reflected in the enormous carved mirror.

An angel decorating the tree with nuts and fruits on Christmas Eve. Often each member of the family had a token gift hanging for them on Christmas day rather than the heaps of wrapped presents underneath that we enjoy today.

Evergreens

People have decorated the house at Christmas for hundreds of years. In early times, people used evergreen foliage such as holly, ivy and rosemary, although it was thought to be unlucky to bring greenery into the house before Yule.

The Kissing Bough, a round bundle of willow branches woven with holly, ivy, mistletoe and yew and hung with apples, was an early form of decoration. There would be a circle of candles under it and people would gather underneath and sing.

Holly

This is probably the most well known seasonal evergreen. The holly, with its prickly leaves and berries, symbolised both the god and goddess to the pagans and was a symbol of eternal life. Later, the Christian Church adopted it as an allusion to the crown of thorns belonging to Jesus, the berries symbolising his blood.

Ivy

Ivy represented good cheer and, when combined with holly, ensured fertility within the house as holly was the spirit of winter and ivy the spirit of summer. In early times it was thought that if ivy grew on the outside walls of the house, it would keep the occupants safe from witches.

Mistletoe

Mistletoe grows best on old apple trees and it was traditionally picked and sold by gypsies.

Mistletoe was banned from some churches because of its association with paganism, as it was sacred to the druids as a symbol of fertility.

Now it has become a symbol of love and mistletoe is used as an innocent excuse for a kiss.

The Christmas Tree or Yule Tree

The Yule tree was adopted by the Christian Church as a symbol of the holy trinity of Father, Son and Holy Spirit, but its foundations stretch way back into European history. Queen Victoria's German husband, Prince Albert, had fond memories of the Christmas trees of his childhood and so they became popular in Britain from the 1840s.

Originally, their branches would have been decorated with natural items and things that came to hand in winter. Early American settlers used garlands of cranberries, while the British used nuts and apples or homemade biscuits and sweetmeats. Often bits of fancy ribbon and scraps of colourful material were saved through the year to tie on to the branches.

Try to keep winter festivities special and remember that it really is the thought that counts.

Winter Feasting

It is hard for us to imagine the excitement and anticipation felt by people in the past when they looked forward to Christmas. They didn't receive anywhere near the number of presents that we get today and the majority of children were given very few toys. However, their Christmas stockings would contain a few delicious treats, such as chocolate, nuts and oranges, which many children only managed to taste once a year.

Christmas dinner really was the culinary highlight of the year for many households and the festive meal and all the trimmings was eagerly awaited.

The preparations started in November when the Christmas pudding and cake were made on Stir-up Sunday, an Anglican term for the last Sunday before the season of Advent. Edible treats were stored up all throughout the year, ready for this special annual feast. Everyone appreciated the food they received and made the most of it as they knew that they wouldn't see the like again for another year.

We can generally eat what we want whenever we want it - but it would be nice if we managed to keep some special treats just for Christmas, because it is only with intense anticipation and longing that you can really enjoy something.

FOR XMAS DAY IN THE MORNING

*That heaps of fun and toys and play,
Don't you wish it could always be XMAS day?*

HALEY.

"Christmas comes but once a year"

The Christmas goose was more common before the popularisation of the turkey and geese would be driven to market from the countryside, often with their webbed feet dipped in tar to prevent them from going lame.

Celebrating Winter...

Make a focal point of the fireplace
Make a cosy corner and watch the flames flicker away

Bring back the art of story-telling
Long ago people gathered by the fire, sharing traditional folklore passed down through the generations – tales of great bravery and heroism, histories of their ancestors and funny memories from childhood. Winter is a great time of year to cuddle up, batten down the hatches and remember people and places from the past.

Play games
Dig out the board games or a pack of cards, play a game of charades or resurrect an old-fashioned party game like blind man's buff. Playing games is often seen as something to amuse children, but in the past the games were for the adults and parlour games of all sorts, often resulting in hilarious laughter, were enjoyed all year round, but especially at Christmas.

Feed the birds
Our poor little bird friends can suffer terribly in cold winters, so get creative in the kitchen and fashion them tasty treats from your leftovers. Keep a tub in the freezer to which you can add left over animal fat from cooking and then when you have enough, pop it in a saucepan, melt it down and add a mix of nuts, fruits, crumbs, grains (the crumbs left at the bottom of packets of breakfast cereals) and whatever else you have to hand. Pour into a mould (a plastic container from your recycling pile will do). Push into it a loop of string and, when it has set hard, hang it outside for the birds to enjoy. Don't forget that birds need a supply of clean fresh water too.

Making and mending
Sort through your mending pile and spend an evening doing the little sewing jobs you have been putting off all year. What can't be mended, put in a rag bag – it may inspire you to start a patchwork quilt of your own.

Make presents
Long winter evenings are a good time to have a go at making presents for friends and family. Or, instead of taking a day off to go Christmas shopping, why not spend a day making your presents instead – far less stressful.

Open your house to family and friends
Grandma's house has been a special place for Christmas for many years – grandparents can indulge as much as they want for they do not have to live with the consequences, which they know all too well.

Start a hobby or learn a new skill
Winter is a great time to start a new hobby. Gather your thoughts together and work out what it is you really enjoy doing. Investigate, research and then do!

Get in touch
Now is the time of year to make contact with family and friends you don't see very often. Send them a card, an email or make a phone call. Write more than the standard season's greetings, tell them about your year and your family, enclose a photo and invite them to visit.

Rest
Many animals go into hibernation during the winter months, so if that is what your body is telling you to do then do it. Nature uses winter to recharge its batteries in readiness to burst into growth in spring – there is no shame in taking it easy, especially if you have a seasonal job.

Make plans
Plan for the year ahead and get your affairs in order. Make a list of things you want to achieve in the next 12 months – what work would you like to do in the house or garden?

Put on a play or a puppet show

THIS GAME IS THE OPPOSITE OF "BLINDMAN'S-BUFF", BECAUSE ALL THE PLAYERS ARE BLINDFOLDED EXCEPT ONE, AND HE MOVES AROUND THE ROOM RINGING A BELL. THE FIRST BLINDFOLDED PLAYER TO CATCH HIM BECOMES THE "JINGLER", WHILST THE FIRST JINGLER IS BLINDFOLDED.

Come to Grandma's for a Merry Christmas

With Best Wishes

Old tins make lovely containers for presents, and save on the need for wrapping paper   just tie with a ribbon.

Decorating for Christmas

Dried cranberries strung onto garden wire and shaped into a heart form a simple festive decoration and afterwards you can hang it outside for the birds to enjoy.

Seek out vintage tea sets and dinner services with gold or silver decorations – they look wonderfully festive and work out much cheaper than the modern ranges found in shops in the run up to Christmas.

This stocking was handmade from remnants of a damaged Welsh blanket, creating something that will become part of the festivities for many years to come.

A Merry Xmas to You.

Though the air is chilly,
May your heart be gay
With the sweetest sunshine,
Of love's golden ray.

A wonderful array of vintage baubles, grouped together in a glass bowl like festive jewels.

Christmas crackers go back to Victorian times when they were used for all celebrations, including Easter and birthdays.

Celebrating the New Year

HAPPY NEW YEAR

JANUARY

A GLAD NEW YEAR

A HAPPY NEW YEAR TO YOU

JANUARY 1

A Happy New Year

Out with the old and in with the new

New Beginnings

As winter comes to an end, the first signs of spring appear. By the end of March, things are well underway and the 21st marks the spring equinox when night and day are equal. This is a time for getting rid of the old and welcoming the new.

In Pagan times, people celebrated the dawn goddess Eostar or Ostara (later developed into the Christian Easter celebration). She was the goddess of fertility in the body, the mind, the land and all living things. Her symbols are the egg and the hare.

This is a great time for change and renewal, so if you want to redecorate your house, then this is a great time to do it.

May Day (Beltane)

On this day masses of spring flowers were brought into the home and it was the only day of the year that May flowers, from the Hawthorn tree, were allowed into the house as they were thought to be unlucky the rest of the year.

A HAPPY EASTER

A springtime table set using vintage green glassware and china. The tablecloth is an old Sanderson fabric with cheery daffodils, which would be perfect for the Welsh St David's Day on the 1st of March.

An Art Deco tea set with green polka dots, perfect for a spring time cuppa.

Daffodils are the brightest harbinger of spring — there are so many varieties, both large and small, some have beautifully fragrant flowers.

With TRUE Affection

Celebrating Spring...

Have a spring clean
Traditionally, this was carried out from the last week in April to the middle of May. At that time of the year it was no longer necessary to light fires in the main living and bedrooms and so the spring clean could remove all the soot and smuts along with the accumulated dust of the year.
Spring cleaning was about more than just scrubbing floors and removing greasy finger marks from furniture, it was an important household chore, which insured a clean, healthy and hygienic home that was free from pests.

The housewife would often have help moving furniture and rolling up carpets so that all parts of every room could be inspected and cleaned. Cracks in walls and floor boards were filled to remove places where insects could hide (they would even use small blow torches to direct flames between the floorboards to kill off any lurking bed bugs). By lifting up carpets and scrubbing the floors underneath, they would catch early infestations of carpet beetles and moths before any real damage was done and a thorough polish of the furniture would keep the pesky woodworm in check. Books were taken off shelves and dusted and checked for bookworms and the pantry was disinfected against mites and roaches.

We may think our homes are free from these sorts of creepy inmates, but they are not and as we start to neglect these sorts of chores in our nice warm houses and make do with the occasional hoover under the bed, we may soon find that insects such as bed bugs (which really do bite) may return.

Open the windows and let the spring air in whenever you can.

Change your heavyweight winter curtains for summer ones to let the light and the warmth of the sun stream in.

Make a focal point of a window seat an area overlooking the garden so you can watch spring bloom.

Welcome spring into your home with a springtime display
Bring flowering twigs into the home. Branches from blackcurrant bushes will continue to sprout leaves and bloom if placed in a vase of water and they have a delicious smell.
Many species of willow will sprout catkins, which will last many weeks indoors. They may even grow roots.

Hold an egg hunt
Eggs are a traditional symbol of springtime and children love romping around the garden and a bit of a competition. So gather as many children as your garden can accommodate together and hold an egg hunt.
From past experience, it is a good idea to count the eggs as you hide them, so you can count them up at the end and see if there are any missing (this is particularly important if you have a pet dog as chocolate is harmful to them and they will think nothing of scoffing as many as they can, wrapper and all).

Host a gardening party
Rather than a garden party where everyone comes to eat, drink and be merry, why not have a gardening party instead? In fact, you and your family and friends could take it in turns to hold a gardening party, and that way everyone can have a garden makeover for the price of a few refreshments. It is so much more fun working with others and this is a great way of helping you with some big gardening tasks such as digging a new border or planting a new hedge.

Little Tommy Tittlemouse.

LITTLE Tommy Tittlemouse
Lived in a little house;
He caught fishes
In other men's
ditches.

A little bunny ornament would take pride of place in any springtime home

A Happy Eastertide

Nicole's spring-themed mantelpiece has beautiful hand-painted wooden eggs, collected over the years, a cute lustreware china rabbit bought in a charity shop for 90p and a display of Edwardian Easter cards. Little vases of spring flowers are added to finish the pretty seasonal display

A cheerful Easter

Nicole's homemade Easter tree is made from a branch of hedgerow blackthorn stood in an old stoneware jar. On it dangle blown out goose eggs from her own geese, which have been decorated by her children along with paper flowers and little wooden ornaments.

Greetings

EASTER GLADNESS

SUMMER

Miniature gardens make lovely summer displays and children will enjoy getting involved too.

A decorative birdcage filled with summer flowers makes a lovely seasonal display in the home.

This is the lightest, warmest and most productive time of the year. During the summer months, the house is often just a place to sleep as most of our living is done outside (well that would be the ideal, but British weather is not always so kind).

The Summer Solstice and the longest day of the year is the 21st of June and this is one of the few ancient Pagan celebrations that is not celebrated by mainstream society today.

In farming communities it is a busy time, with weeks of picking and harvesting crops.

Making the Most of Summer...

Let the sunshine in.
Replacing thick, dark winter curtains with pale and light materials such as muslin or lace will let the sun's rays flood into your home, allowing you to make the most of summer.

Decorate your home with flowers
If your garden has an abundance of summer flowers, use them to decorate the dinner table. You don't have to wait for a special occasion, even dinner for one is more cheery if you are sitting next to a vase of beautiful blooms.

Seasonal displays
Summer displays will remind you of past holidays and future trips. A trip to the seaside to see the boats is an important summer event.

Relax and make the most of the sunshine.
Take a holiday, go on a day trip or just sit in the garden and watch the bees at work. Give your body a chance, turn the sun's rays into vitamin D to help you stay healthy through the dark winter months.

Cup cakes are like a taste of summer. Strawberry cupcakes, topped with strawberry butter-icing and finished with a fresh strawberry on top.

A MERRY SEASON

INVITATION

INVI

Let's have a party

We are having a Party
on SATURDAY next – 21st inst
from 4 PM till 8 PM o'clock
and will be so pleased if you will come.
To: JUNE & JANET
FROM: AUDREY SIMMONS R.S.

Celebrate today, for tomorrow we may die...

We all know that we cannot live forever, but few of us really live for today. In the past, people were more aware of their own mortality and how quickly loved ones could be lost, through war, dangerous working conditions or sickness. Although it's a depressing thought, it made people appreciate those around them and make the most of any time they had. Family, friends and neighbours shared each others ups and downs and enjoyed themselves when they could. Special occasions were often simple affairs, knowing that good company is all that is really needed for a good time.

Your home should be a centre for all sorts of celebrations

"The gathering of one's friends is the happiest part of home life."
The Ideal Home c1912

OLD DAYS COME BACK TO MEMORY

HAPPY DAYS

SOMETHING TO LOOK BACK ON

Celebrate whenever you can — open your house and share it with everyone.

For it is these memories, which will keep you when you are old. Those happy days when you loved and laughed will flood back when you most need them.

What happens to you in your home and the feelings it inspires in you and others is more important than how perfectly it is decorated and how much money it cost.

No one can take away your memories or spoil them, and they can become a comfort in old age and illness.

When You've A Guest

SHARE YOUR HOME WITH OTHERS

Make time to get to know people – you never know where you will find a friend.

Inviting people to afternoon tea may seem a little old fashioned, but it is a good way of welcoming people you don't know so well into your home.

Having guests doesn't mean your house will be overrun. You can gather in just one room (and the rest of the house can be a mess – they need never know). Good old-fashioned hospitality is not about showing off your best china and table cloths, but it does express a level of care and thought towards your guests, show that you have taken the time to make a special effort and that you appreciate their company. However, it is lovely to have an occasion to get out your special bits and pieces and to take pleasure in using them and sharing them with others.

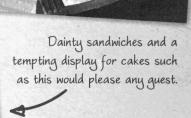

Scones, jam and clotted cream are a special afternoon tea treat to share.

Dainty sandwiches and a tempting display for cakes such as this would please any guest.

Beautiful family china, linen napkins and a lace tablecloth are a delight to use for both host and guest.

LADIES "AT HOME" AROUND 1900.

Middle Class ladies at the turn of the century would often host a weekly gathering of friends and neighbours known as At Home, a couple of hours in the afternoon when guests could drop by for a cup of tea and a chat and know that they were not imposing on their hostess. Our lives are far less formal today, and often friends will pop in at anytime, but what about those we don't know so well? Wouldn't it be wonderful to reintroduce a similar event today so that new neighbours or new friends could be made to feel welcome?

True happiness consists of making others happy.

Here's to the Birthday we celebrate!

For Mother's Birthday
Like the moonbeam's silvery rays for brightness
Like the sunshine on the flowers for brightness
So I wish dear Mother be the pleasure
That this Birthday bless you in rich measure.

FOR MY HUSBAND'S BIRTHDAY.
May every sunrise bring anew
Pleasures of the past to you,
And every sunset tell of more
New and happier Joys in store.

A pretty outdoor tea,
even shop-bought cakes
look special on such
lovely vintage china.

Cake making and decoration was taken very seriously by many housewives in the 1950s and the fashion was for elaborate and colourful icing.

Facing page 30.

1. Family Cake.
2. Mocha Cake.
3. Chocolate Ginger Cake.
4. Yuletide Cake.
5. Butter Cream Tarts.

You can easily add your own little decorations to ready-made cakes to make them extra special.

A special effort for a birthday tea, using mismatched vintage china and glassware.

CONGRATULATIONS ON YOUR 21ST BIRTHDAY

Sincere Good Wishes

May the springtime of your life be bright Dear friend of mine And age come softly like a summer's night With thoughts divine

I would be very glad if you came to my birthday party

on

at

Many Happy Returns to Mother.

Just to WISH You Many Happy RETURNS of the Day.

A Birthday wish for every gladness May love and happiness entwined Bring you years of every pleasure, Health and best of Luck combined.

There's no love like a Mothers', So take my Birthday Greeting, God send you joy and happiness, And grant your cares be fleeting.

Nicole's first ever attempt at cake decorating. The cake's a bit wonky and the ready-to-roll icing decorations very amateur but the effort and sentiment was much appreciated by her friend Sam.

A Birthday Wish

May all the scenes around you Be filled with Heaven's own light And may all joys combine

A set of vintage shot glasses would make a great 18th or 21st birthday present.

I've just heard the good news!

WHITE HEATHER FOR LUCK

WITH HEARTIEST CONGRATULATIONS ON YOUR ENGAGEMENT.

There's no end to a ring, may there be none to your happiness.

Presents

It was perfectly acceptable years ago for people to give second-hand presents and to receive with great appreciation family treasures and heirlooms. So have a think about what you can give, whether it's for a wedding, christening, birthday or anniversary. Find something with real meaning, which they wouldn't be able to buy themselves. You may have a family patchwork quilt, a vintage Welsh blanket, or a useful piece of furniture such as a pine blanket box – everyone will appreciate something beautiful and useful given with thought.

A vintage picnic set in original condition would make a wonderful wedding present with a difference

FRED R J WAITE   late Waite & Pettitt   CENTRAL STUDIO

FRED R J WAITE   late Waite & Pettitt   CENTRAL STUDIO CHELTENHAM

UNTIL DEATH WILL SEPERATE.

Best Wishes
on your
WEDDING
DAY

HERE ARE CONGRATULATIONS
FOR A VERY HAPPY PAIR!
SWEETER THAN ORANGE BLOSSOMS
BE THE JOYS YOU TWO WILL SHARE.

Heartiest
Congratulations

Borrowed pieces of garden furniture, tables and chairs are spread out in the garden, so there is always a comfortable place to sit.

Big Celebrations at Home

If you have the space (and good weather) then there is nothing more special than hosting big family celebrations at home. If you call in favours from family and friends, you will have a wonderful day that everyone will remember at the fraction of the cost of hiring a venue.

Save the petals from drooping roses and other colourful flowers and dry them to make your own confetti or scatter onto tables.

A tempting table set with traditional sweets is left for the children to help themselves – well it is a party after all!

Homemade bunting creates an instant party feel

Baskets filled with old Welsh blankets are left out for guests to spread out on the grass and enjoy the sunshine.

Tables set in the garden with vintage tea sets borrowed from family and friends. The tables are decorated with jugs of wild flowers

The drinks table is set so that guests can help themselves.

An activity table, with puzzles or colouring books, will help keep children occupied especially if there are to be long speeches.

Hosting a Dinner Party

Holding a dinner party is a great way of sharing your home and your friends with a wider circle of people you would like to know better. It is also a great excuse to get friends and family together for grown-up time away from children. It doesn't have to be a formal affair, although sometimes it's nice to have an excuse to use the dining room for its proper use and really push the boat out a bit.

Get out the best china (or borrow some), dust down the crystal glasses, granny's table linen and the family silver. Whatever lovely bits and pieces you have for entertaining, get them out and use them. A dinner party is a lovely grown-up way of celebrating a birthday or anniversary, but you don't have to wait for a special occasion — wanting to gather people together in order enjoy each other's company is a motive enough.

Themed dinner parties, such as a murder mystery or a casino night, are great fun. Or you can theme a party around a country, such as India or Italy, or even use a decade such as the 1960s, using music and food to create the atmosphere. Fancy dress is optional, but always fun.

Opening your home for entertaining doesn't mean you have to meet all of the costs. Everyone will be grateful for the invitation and more than happy to pitch in. In the past family and friends shared the burden, with each bringing a dish and contributions to the occasion.

Why not host a pot luck party and ask each guest to bring a dish? This works especially well with themed meals such as a curry night, where each guest brings a different curry and the host supplies the rice, naan bread and poppadoms.

An Edwardian dinner table set with beautiful summer flowers, Cassells Household Guide 1912.

A lavish Victorian table set for dinner party, from Mrs Beeton's Book of Household Management 1899.

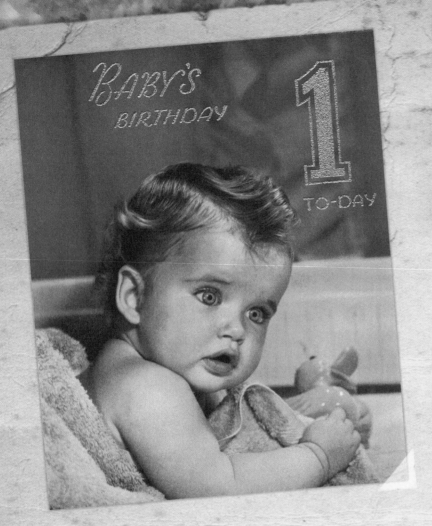

BABY'S BIRTHDAY 1 TO-DAY

Congratulations to Mother and Baby

Congratulations.

We're told, a cherub baby
Has come to live with you
And we send congratulations
To you and baby too.
For nothing else can do so much
To make a home complete
And teach the joy of living
As a baby sound and sweet.

Address Book

CONGRATULATIONS

TO YOU AND YOUR DEAR BABY

Baby

Simple pleasures of childhood
– a homemade swing in a tree

Celebrate today for tomorrow they will be all grown up

making a magical childhood

Tea in the garden

Teach children how to dance

A game of hide and seek

Hours of fun in a sand pit

Simple role-playing games like doctors and nurses delight small children

Allow children to use your home to play. Help them to foster their imaginations by encouraging them to make dens and role-play using everyday things and bits of furniture

Children should have as many happy memories of home as possible. When they look back on their childhood, they won't necessarily remember the new matching duvet set or their expensive computer games, but they will remember the time they helped to paint a tree on their bedroom wall or spent the afternoon having a picnic on the living room floor when it poured with rain outside.

The best thing you can give your children is time and do something creative and imaginative. Teach them to play card games, keep a chessboard or jigsaw puzzle out at all times, make a garden or sweet shop from modeling clay.

Happiness comes from investing time, not money.

When the world wearies

And society cease to satisfy

There is always the garden

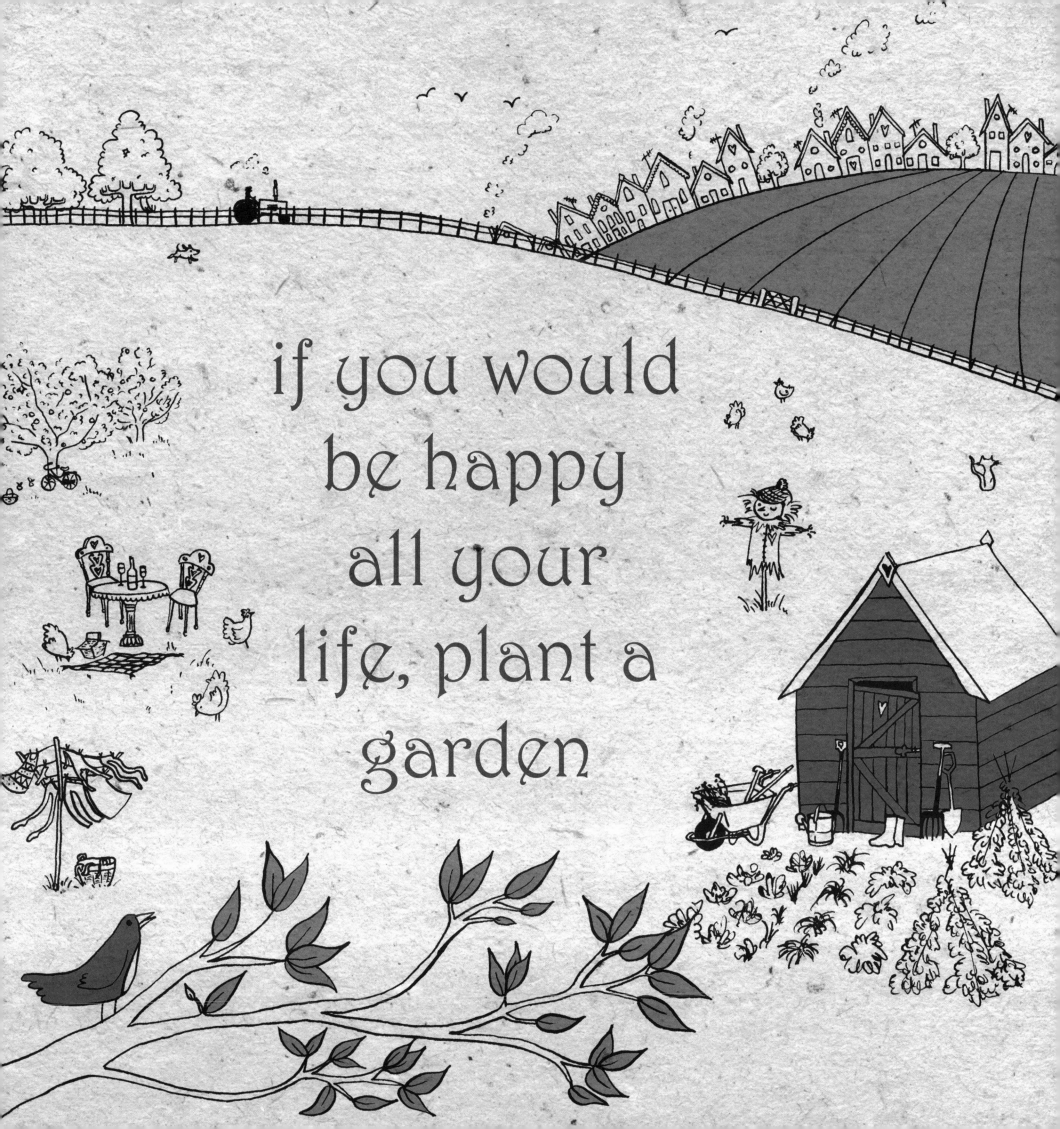

A fragrant rose covered archway leading to a cottage garden

An idyllic cottage garden with roses and hollyhocks.

People who never get outside cannot thrive.

We are all natural beings and part of this earth. We get our energy from plants and animals and our bodies need light and fresh air to survive. Planting a garden can put us back in touch with the very essence of life on this planet, the wonders of nature, the changing of the seasons and the miracle of new growth.

It can also save us money, help us to preserve the planet's precious resources, support local wildlife, provide a healthy diet and allow us to heal ourselves. But, most important of all, planting a garden will almost certainly make us happy.

Almost every culture considers the garden as a private sanctuary away from the hustle and bustle of everyday life, one which gives you an opportunity to create the world of your dreams.

With a patch of soil, some water and a little sunshine, anyone can create their own piece of paradise to be proud of, no matter how small.

If You Would Be Happy All Your Life, Plant a Garden

A proud Edwardian showing off his house and garden.

Beautiful landscaped garden of a large country house

Home Gardening. No. 368. March 23, 1935. [Registered at the G.P.O. as a Newspaper.]

FREE! Chrysanthemum Seeds

HOME GARDENING

2d.

No.368, VOL.15
MAR. 23, 1935

For thousands of years, humans have crafted themselves little sections of order amongst the wilderness. Some gardens were status symbols of the wealthy; others were a source of food or income, a productive space that was vital to the survival of the families tending them.

There are many reasons for having a garden...

As an Extension of the House: A space in which to enjoy the sunshine while relaxing, eating and entertaining outside or cooking over a bonfire on an autumn evening.

A Play Area: Somewhere for the family to run, jump, hide, dig, kick a ball and daydream.

A Place for Pets: Somewhere for a dog to run around and for children to look after animals.

A Lovely Aspect: A pretty view from the kitchen window and a chance to bring the great outdoors into your home

A Source of Fresh Flowers: Your own personal cutting garden for the house

To Feed Your Family: Fruit, vegetables, eggs and herbs, providing either all or part of the fresh produce on your table

Healing: Herbs and medicinal plants to make home cures and remedies.

Supporting Nature: Looking after the local birds, animals and insects by providing somewhere to live and find food.

Household Chores: Drying washing, carpet beating, cleaning, polishing and mending.

A Storage Space: Somewhere to site the garage, shed or outbuilding, keeping gardening equipment, tools, bikes, outside toys and general overflow away from the house.

A Place of Peace and Quiet: Somewhere to be still, to read, to meditate and just to be.

GARDENING CAN BE HARD, PHYSICAL WORK, BUT HAS MANY REWARDS

There are many uses for reclaimed bricks in the garden — never turn down the opportunity to acquire more. They make great raised beds, paths, garden walls, ponds — the list is endless.

Making a Pretty Nostalgic Garden

It is never too early to encourage children to help with the garden, this little girl is eager to help with the watering

You can apply the same principles to making a garden as you would to making a home:

- Be grateful for what you already have and focus on the positives.

- Waste nothing and think creatively.

- Do things as well as you can or find someone who can do them for you.

- Appreciate the garden's beauty as well as it's usefulness.

- Be bold, and don't be afraid to experiment.

- Live by the seasons and respect the power of nature.

- Do a little well and often to keep on top of things.

- Share your garden with people you love.

A traditional vegetable patch laid out ready for planting and sowing seed in rows

This garden fence has been made out of whatever was to hand — fencing wire, old branches, pallets and even a cartwheel

These half-sawn logs make a sturdy path and also a good habitat for lots of insects

The Edible Garden

It is amazingly satisfying to be able to grow your own food. You may not see yourself as a gardener – perhaps you think you don't have the time or the skills – but just have a go.

You would need a garden of about half an acre in order to grow all the fruit and vegetables needed to feed a small family. Few of us have gardens of that size, but it is possible to grow something edible in whatever space you have, even if it's just a parsley garnish for your homemade pasta dish.

Not all vegetables are high maintenance – many varieties have high yields yet need little input from us. Simply scatter a handful of radish seeds in a sunny spot and you'll be picking crops within just a few weeks.

Fruit is generally easy to grow in your own garden. Soft fruit such as blackcurrant grow on small bushes, with pretty fragrant flowers in early spring. With a little pruning, they could provide enough fruit for around 10 pots of jam (enough to see most families through the year) as well as some left over for pies and crumbles.

Fruit trees require a bit more space but many, such as plums and pears, grow tall and straight so don't take up much room in the garden. If space is an issue, you could plant a mixed fruit tree, where an apple and pear or different varieties of each are grafted to form the one tree, giving you more variety from the same space.

...a young forest garden, with vegetables, herbs ...rawberries all growing under a fruit tree.

...ptural, beautifully coloured and ...tasty, this oriental salad is a ...l vegetable for a small garden.

This is a forest garden, a system of mixed planting where trees, shrubs and ground cover share and benefit from the same space. This is how plants would grow if nature was allowed free reign. It is low maintenance and allows you to gather lots of different crops from a small space.

A Cox's eating apple ripening in the sun – it is wonderful to just help yourself to your own fruit straight from the tree

Don't be too hasty in clearing the weeds from your garden – this blackberry bush and elder tree self-seeded near the fence and now provide an abundance of free food. You can use the elderflowers, which bloom in June to make cordial and wine then, later in the year, use the elderberries and blackberries in delicious crumbles, pies and a million other things. They also provide valuable food and shelter to local wildlife and provide a touch of natural landscape in a suburban garden.

A tree dripping with Victoria Plums – a glut such as this needs attention before it goes to waste. If you don't have time to eat them or preserve them yourself, then swap and share with others – they may pay you back later in the year with other garden goodies you don't grow yourself.

Swiss Chard is easy to grow and hardy once it gets going. You can use it in many dishes and, with its colourful leaves, it could easily slot in to any flower-bed.

A Grenadier Cooking Apple – this tree is on a dwarf rootstock so takes up very little room. Its lush green fruit ripens earlier than most in the summer so you can enjoy apple crumbles anytime from July.

There are so many pears on this branch that it is about to snap. Pick a few of the pears early and allow the rest to grow on and use them to make thinning jam (a traditional jam made from a jumble of overcrowded fruit, which is picked from the fruit trees to allow the remaining fruit to grow larger)– nothing should go to waste.

fragrance, flavour and healing

Your garden can be a very sensual place – providing beautiful scented plants to enjoy on a summer's evening or to make into potpourri, culinary herbs to add variety to your home cooked food and even flowers and leaves you can use to treat yourself, your family and even your pets for a whole range of ailments and problems.

Sage has evergreen leaves and is a vital ingredient in lots of dishes including sage and onion stuffing. Infusing the leaves in boiling water makes a useful gargle for sore throats.

The intense perfume of honeysuckle drifts through the garden on a summer's evening

This calendula (or pot marigold) has vibrant orange daisy-like flowers. Often called poor man's saffron, its petals are edible and look wonderful in salads. They make a vivid yellow natural dye and have soothing and antiseptic properties.

English lavender, with its sweet clean smell, can keep insects and moths away, is a powerful antiseptic and helps reduce stress and induce a good night's sleep.

Peppermint not only smells wonderful, it can be used to make mint sauce for your lamb dinner and mint tea to help calm your stomach and aid digestion. Be careful though as its roots are invasive and it will spread wildly if not contained.

Thyme, with its tiny fragrant leaves, can be used to flavour lots of dishes and you can grow these dense, low growing plants closely together to form an aromatic carpet.

An Edwardian lady in her cutting garden. Leaving a bit of room among your vegetables to grow flowers and foliage for cutting can give you a year-round display for your home and the perfect gift for family and friends.

Old roses are wonderfully decorative and one of the best herbal plants – they can be used in cooking, cosmetics, medicine and crafts. Use the petals in desserts, in jams, as a tea and in potpourri. The red rose hips or fruit of the rose are rich in Vitamin C and make delicious syrup and jams.

A border from a physic garden

GARDEN FRIENDS

You can share your garden with a host of garden friends, some of whom are better behaved than others.

Some, such as chickens, ducks and geese, might well prove useful while others, such as dogs and cats, are adored but can be a nuisance in the garden. Try to get the balance right and allow all to enjoy and benefit from the garden.

CHICKENS

Chickens are amazing creatures and brilliant additions to a garden. They need little apart from somewhere to roost at night and keep them safe from Mr Fox (who recently killed six of Nicole's chickens!), some layers pellets, corn and fresh water. They are happy to roam free around your garden, but you may be happier restricting them to a small run as they are relentless scratchers and scavengers.

Sarah's chicken is using an unused raised bed as a dust bath. In this case it is doing good — by scratching around, eating weed seeds and slug eggs and leaving droppings, it is improving the soil ready for planting. However, it would be a different story if this bed was freshly planted or sown with seed.

WHILE·THE·CHICKENS·IN·THE·GARDEN
KEEP·SCRATCHING·ALL·THE·TIME
I·THOUGHT·YOU'D·LIKE·TO·HEAR·FROM·ME
SO·I'LL·SCRATCH·YOU·JUST·A·LINE

This large lawn has somewhere for dogs, children and grown-ups to play

Ducks are great fun, but messy, so don't keep them if you are particularly garden proud.

A quiet garden friend, whose sole purpose is to make people happy

Cats, both yours and your neighbours', will come and go as they please — they are free spirits, garden friends and also great garden enemies. They leave unwanted and unhealthy piles of poo and also scare away and prey on lots of local wildlife.

A homemade fire pit in Helen's back garden — used for cooking but also by her sons, who spend hours around the fire at all times of the year toasting marshmallows.

Nicole's two boys use the garden to play, by building fortresses, castles and rocky coves from the stones they find lying around.

This reclaimed stone seat has been recently built but it looks as if it has been apart of the garden forever. What a lovely place to read a book or to just sit and think.

This bell tent creates a great outdoor living space and can be kept up all through the summer (as long as the wind isn't too strong) to provide an extra living area, a children's den or, here, as a meditation area.

Live in your garden as you would the rest of the house and treat it as an extra room - outdoor living can recharge even the dullest personal battery.

In years gone by before the invention of specialist garden and patio furniture, they would just drag any table outside the back door to enjoy afternoon tea in the sunshine.

A stone patio is perfect for a simple game of hopscotch.

A stone barbecue in Brett and Wayne's garden, built by Brett from local stone.

A small seating area in the shade of a weeping damson tree.

When you're planning your garden, it pays to focus on the future. Aim to at least preserve the world as it is now and if possible try to make up for the natural spaces which have been lost over the year.

If you take something from nature, try to put something else back in its place. So if you dig up your lawn to lay a con—crete patio, try to give something back to nature in return, such as planting a native hedge around it.

Make long term investments such as planting trees. Oak takes decades to mature and it may not fruit within your own lifetime, but future generations will appreciate and enjoy it at its prime.

Look after the earth's resources and conserve water wherever you can — use water butts and rain harvesting systems to collect and store water to use on the garden, or divert waste water from the house to your vegetables.

The beginnings of a brand new woodland — this three-year-old ash sapling has been planted alongside 50 others and within four or five years they can be coppiced for firewood or just left to grow into magnificent trees. Ash is ideal for firewood as you can burn it green. If you don't have room to plant a woodland in your garden then try at least to plant a few trees or long-living shrubs as your present to the future.

A novel planter made from an old pair of jeans

A rustic water storage system, using an old coopered barrel.

Gardening for the future

The Victorians were keen on window box gardening. As this picture shows, you can create a lovely display even in the shade.

WINDOW WITH A SHADY ASPECT.

Make full use of a window ledge — this one has a display of low maintenance conifer and ivy, with winter pansies for colour.

You can grow many things on the side of a house — this wisteria makes good use of a sunny aspect, but you can also train fruit trees to grow against the walls.

Gardening Without a Garden

You can still have a garden, even if you have no land to dig. Use whatever space you do have to full advantage — plant up containers and use vertical spaces and any nooks and crannies you can find.

A London window garden makes the best possible use of space and creates a haven of colour and beauty in the middle of the city.

This pretty display was found growing in an old stone garden wall.

These Brussels sprouts have been grown especially for Christmas. With a similar pot planted with parsnips and carrots, you could grow much of your Christmas dinner even without a garden.

146

Greetings

the nature garden

Wildlife will come and go as it pleases in your garden but, if you make it welcome, it can be as beneficial to you as it is for the birds and the insects.

You can create a balance in your garden, natural predators which thrive will keep down the damage caused by garden pests without the use of nasty chemicals.

Squirrels are frequent garden visitors; they can be a nuisance but have to be admired for their cleverness and ingenuity

Bees need all the help they can get nowadays, so plant flowers they love, such as this verbena.

The beautiful berries of the cotoneaster are very decorative and loved by birds.

Don't be too tidy. By leaving logs such as this around the garden, you are providing the perfect habitat for many insects.

Rowan berries are much appreciated by birds in the cold days of winter. If there is enough to go around, they make a good jelly too.

Butterflies are great garden friends and good plant pollinators, but beware the cabbage whites and keep your brassicas covered or your veg will be teaming with caterpillars before you know it.

Some wildlife needs keeping in check and this glass wasp trap filled with sugary water is a safe way of stopping a garden invasion from the not-so-friendly visitor.

R42/4

Gloria

HOUSE KEEPING FOR THE PRETTY NOSTALGIC HOME

There is lots of useful advice to be found in the housekeeping manuals of the past and many hints and tips, which can prove useful today. Of course, we do not have an army of domestic help to keep our modern homes in order.

"One of the greatest virtues that can adorn a cottage is a homely pride in the cleanliness, purity and health of the household."

Sylvia's Book of Family Management c1880.

A beautiful antique pine chest of drawers not shown off to its best advantage in my younger son's bedroom.

An example of the clutter left by me not putting my things away — piles such as this get moved from surface to surface until an avalanche happens or visitors are expected and then they get put away

A once lovely bunch of daffodils, left decaying in a vase in my kitchen – not so pretty now!

I have to be honest here and admit that I am not a naturally tidy person. As a child I had a messy bedroom and no amount of nagging or bribery would encourage me to keep it any other way. My home today lurches from stressed neatness (normally when visitors are expected), to an embarrassing state of clutter, with nothing in between.

My natural state of homely chaos is even more remarkable when you consider that I have been fascinated by domestic history since I was a teenager, that I started collecting antique cookery books and household management manuals whilst at university and that I worked as curator and domestic history historian and have amassed a vast collection of domestic equipment from the past.

I have recently taken on some paid help to share the burden, but I've come to realise it is very difficult for anybody to clean between so much general untidiness and that I have a considerable amount of sorting and organising to do before my lovely cleaner can clean properly.

I have written this chapter for my benefit and for others like me — people who love stuff, collect everything, organise nothing, never put their toys away and, quite frankly, would rather do anything than housework. I hereby swear an oath to start practicing what I preach and get myself and my family into a housekeeping regime because I want to keep my Pretty Nostalgic Home, and all the lovely things in it, looking nice and my family happy (although they will not be getting off scot-free).

Much of the advice, suggestions and ideas in this book will be fruitless if your home is badly managed. You don't necessarily need a spotlessly tidy house, but a well-balanced, homely space, maintained equally by the whole family, will help create a welcoming home where you can relax, share experiences and feel proud.

I've collated housekeeping advice from Edwardian and Victorian households — some tips are just as relevant today as they ever were, other pieces of advice you might find won't fit in with your lifestyle. Take what you think will work for you and integrate it into your home.

Nicole x

Come Into the Parlour

ORATION.

In the working class homes of the past, the parlour was the best room kept for high days, holidays and special visitors. It was always in perfect condition and it would not be used by members of the family at any other time. This meant that large families were cramped into the kitchen-cum-living room for their everyday living. Although this seems like wasted space, the principle of having one room always kept tidy and special is sensible, especially if you have more than one reception room. It would really take the pressure off unexpected visits if you always had a clean and tidy room available in which to entertain.

In our home we employ a one-in one-out toy policy and it is the first room to receive attention on the cleaning round. If you have one well-kept room then visitors might assume that the rest of your house is the same. Of course, we let close friends into our inner sanctum of chaos, but even these friend would appreciate somewhere to chat without sitting on broken toys and doggy dribble.

1.
House keeping is a worthy job

"When a woman says she is a housewife, she should say it with the utmost pride, for there is nothing higher on this planet to which she could aspire"

John Seymour, Forgotten Household Crafts 1987

At first this quote seems condescending to women – why can't they aspire to be Prime Minister, or a CEO of a global company? But, rather than downgrading the aspirations or abilities of women, who are obviously capable of doing whatever job they choose, I think this quote is about upgrading and recognising the importance of good housekeeping and household management. The term housewife or house husband has become a dirty word. But I think that whoever chooses to maintain a home, male or female, should feel rightfully proud of their task, for it is as worthy as any profession.

"A happy home, efficiently conducted is a garden where young lives are reared to noble issues, and no home is happy that is not well managed"

Sylvia's Book of Family Management c1880.

If you can do a little well – look after your home by keeping it clean, organised, comfortable, well maintained and beautiful for those who share it with you – then you will be doing much more than you realise. Being a housewife or husband is not a menial role, and society would benefit greatly if more people were willing to take on the role seriously rather than letting the house fend for itself.

A well run home lays the foundations for a happy family

In the past, housekeeping was the sole responsibility of the wife. However, the liberation of women has allowed them to leave their posts in droves, and go off to do something more interesting instead. But nobody has come to replace them and homes all over the country have virtual signs hanging in their front window - housekeeper wanted - situation vacant.

2.
Housekeeping is the responsibility of the whole family

Everyone living in the house should share responsibility for its upkeep, but all too often you see an over-worked mother struggling to keep up with a job and the housework, while other members of the family watch and look on.

We need to stop thinking of housekeeping as drudgery and treat it as a worthwhile activity, which adds value to family life.

Even though women managed the house in the past, they didn't do all of the work. Many had paid domestic help and most families gave children chores to carry out before they were allowed to play. Men often contributed by carrying coal, making, mending and repairing, gardening and growing food as well as painting and decorating. Nobody had time to sit idly by.

Today, housekeeping should be a joint effort but there must be a system of work in place. There could be an appointed household manager, who works out the plan and what needs to be done and then delegates roles and responsibilities to others, or there could be a committee system where everyone has a part in decision making.

You could get more labour-saving devices or even pay a cleaner to help out, but neither of these will make a home for you – only you and your family can turn your house into a home.

So have a family meeting to work out what sort of home you want to live in and what jobs need to be done in order to achieve it – then make sure everyone contributes towards it. If everyone does a little well, the family as a whole will do much.

3.
A plan of work

Our homes cannot possibly have the strict standards and routines of those served by many servants a hundred years ago and homeowners today would not possibly comply with the laborious housekeeping regimes of the 1930's housewife. Even so, we should aim for some routine in our modern day homes because, even with our advantages of modern technology, wondrous cleaning products and more relaxed social attitudes, it is still very true that without order, there will be chaos.

With little time to dedicate to housekeeping, our homes can quickly become chaotic. By having a general de-clutter, doing little bits of cleaning here and there and never really doing anything well, we barely scratch the surface of what needs doing.

Make a plan of all the jobs that need doing every day, every week and every month along with special things that the family can do as a treat when the jobs have been done.

Creating a homely home

It's difficult to be happy in a house in which you are so ashamed of the clutter that you can't invite friends inside but neither can you relax in a home where you are constantly on guard and worried about making a mess. Aim to create a balanced and homely house, neither too spic-and-span nor too messy. This is perhaps easier said than done but there are many golden nuggets of advice passed down to us from the past, which can help.

4.
A place for everything and everything in its place

Make sure you have enough storage for everything you need. If you don't need something, it performs no role or you don't love it then get it out of the house (give it away, sell it or recycle it).

Bit by bit, re-organise your storage so that everything has a home. How many of us have drawers so full of stuff that we never used them and we are not even sure what is in them? Sort them out, putting things that make sense together.

Use old suitcases, blanket boxes and ottomans as extra storage space for everything from DVDs to winter blankets. Be inventive with your storage and you can even make a feature out of them.

Stop clutter - less is more
Do your children really need that many toys? Do they even know exactly what they have? If they have fewer toys then they will get more fun out of what they have and will use their imagination to fill in any gaps.

5.
Keeping up the good work

Tidy up as you go along
There is a difference between keeping your home clean and keeping it tidy – if you don't keep it tidy then it is impossible to keep it clean. A quick spruce up a few times a day will mean that when you need to do some cleaning, you can get to the surfaces and do it in half the time.

Do not allow items to clutter and congregate. As soon as one item is left on a chair, then it is a free-for-all and it will soon be joined by other bits and bobs.

Have a basket at the bottom of the stairs to take things that belong upstairs up, but don't leave items in the basket – actually put them away.

Personal responsibility
If everyone in the house were made fully responsible for their own possessions and their own mess, then it would be much easier to keep the house tidy. Children in the past were instilled with this idea from birth – all toys had to be put back in their original boxes and put away nicely into the toy box or cupboard when they were finished with and certainly before another multi-piece game was emptied out onto the floor. It was also expected that their possessions would be put back into order and tidied away before mealtimes and at bedtime. If something was lost or broken, it would not be automatically replaced and toys that were not looked after would be confiscated.

Keep on top of things
Try not to let jobs go undone for too long or it will take more time and effort to get back on track again and a quick wipe down will be turned into a strenuous scrubbing session.

Whistle while you work
Sing, dance, listen to energetic music or do whatever it takes to keep energy levels up until the work is done. Children work very well to music and in nursery schools they often have 'tidy up time' music and as soon as it's played the kids jump to it and start putting toys away. This could be adapted for any home and it's amazing how much tidying can be done in the time it takes for even one song track to play.

A spoonful of sugar helps the medicine go down
Rewards for a good job done are very motivating for everyone, whether it's a sweet treat, pocket money, sitting down to watch a favourite film, a game of Scrabble or a trip out with friends. Everyone loves to live in a clean and tidy house and, with the right incentives, every chore will be accomplished easily.

Pretty Nostalgic Manifesto

We are Pretty Nostalgic
We are about:

P Passionate people making a difference
R Reusing the past to make a beautiful present
E Ensuring an ethical approach to everything we do
T Traditional values at out core
T Taking pride in the best Britain has to offer
Y Youthfulness being nothing to do with age

N Never compromising on our standards
O Only promoting British makers and products.
S Sustainable ways of living and working
T Teaching old skills in a new way
A Appreciating what we have
L Loving what we do
G Giving as well as taking
I Independent and beholden to nothing and no-one
C Celebrating life — it is wonderful!

Join Pretty Nostalgic
You can join us in our mission to bring Pretty Nostalgic living to Britain. We are looking for like-minded individuals and Independent shops and business to sell Pretty Nostalgic books, magazines and merchandise.

Be a Pretty Nostalgic Pioneer
We want to recruit a nationwide team of Pretty Nostalgic Pioneers' to work with us. We want our Pioneers to make the money from selling our products and not big multinational companies.
We want our products to be sold by people who care and who share our core values and in turn we want to reward them with a fair share of profits.

We want our Pioneers to be creative people, Artists, Makers, Bakers, Crafters, Growers, Restorers, and Sewers, or vintage or antique dealers. To help support our Pioneers in their own personal businesses and help them to achieve their own business goals.

By being a Pretty Nostalgic Pioneer, you are free to sell as much or as little as you please. You can sell our stock alongside your own, as long as your items are handmade, by you or someone in the UK, or are antique, vintage or second-hand.

Stock Pretty Nostalgic in Your Shop.
We would like to work directly with British independent shopkeepers and not big distribution companies or wholesalers. If you have a shop and believe in the Pretty Nostalgic brand and what we stand for, then please get in touch.

Sarah@prettynostalgic.co.uk

THE MOTHER TOOK THE STRIPS OF GRASS BETWEEN HER FINGERS LIGHT.

THE CHILDREN ROUND THE GARDEN MARCHED, TO THE BEATING OF THEIR DRUM,
WITH LILY FLOWERS FOR FLAGS AND SWORDS: THEY WERE HAVING SPLENDID FUN!

CHICKEN CREAMS

PIGEON PIE

SAVOURY GAME JELLY

CHICKEN AND
GREEN PEAS
En CASSEROLE

ROAST
WILD DUCK